ESSENTIAL MANAGERS

UNDERSTANDING ACCOUNTS

STEPHEN BROOKSON

A Dorling Kindersley Book

LONDON, NEW YORK, MUNICH,
MELBOURNE, DELHI

Managing Editor Adèle Hayward
Series Art Editor Jamie Hanson

DTP Designer Julian Dams, Amanda Peers
Production Controller Michelle Thomas

Senior Managing Editor Stephanie Jackson
Senior Managing Art Editor Nigel Duffield

Produced for Dorling Kindersley by
Cooling Brown
9–11 High Street, Hampton
Middlesex TW12 2SA

Creative Director Arthur Brown
Senior Editor Amanda Lebentz
Editor Helen Ridge

First published in Great Britain in 2001
by Dorling Kindersley Limited,
80 Strand, London WC2R ORL
A Penguin Company

2 4 6 8 10 9 7 5 3

A CIP catalogue record for this book is available from the British Library

ISBN 0-7513-1216-9

Reproduced by Colourscan, Singapore
Printed in China by Wing King Tong

See our complete catalogue at

www.dk.com

CONTENTS

Measuring Performance

Broadening Your Knowledge

INTRODUCTION

Finance is probably the most important function in any organization, and an understanding of the fundamental figures and financial statements is key to successful management. Understanding Accounts *shows you how to master the language of finance, enabling you to contribute more effectively to overall business performance and improve your leadership skills. This book clearly explains how accounts are compiled and shows you how to uncover a wealth of information about financial activity within your own, or a competitor's, organization. Packed with helpful hints, 101 tips, real-life case studies, and practical advice and information, it provides an indispensable guide to using and interpreting a set of accounts.*

UNDERSTANDING THE BASICS

Accounts are produced periodically to measure how well an organization is performing. Learn how they are prepared and what they reveal about your own, or a competitor's, business.

EXPLAINING ACCOUNTS

A set of accounts provides an invaluable insight into business performance. Learn what the three key financial statements are and how they link together to give an overall picture of just how well an organization is faring.

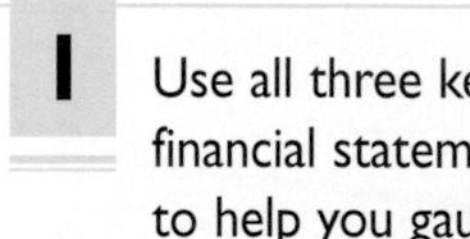

1 Use all three key financial statements to help you gauge corporate success.

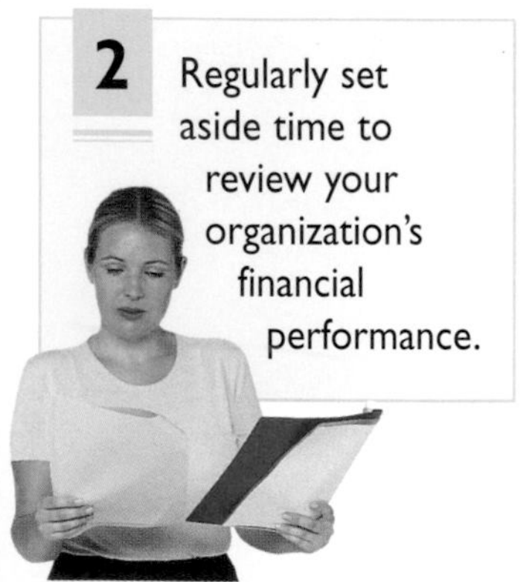

2 Regularly set aside time to review your organization's financial performance.

PRODUCING RELIABLE ACCOUNTS

When Italian monk Fra Pacioli first invented double-entry bookkeeping some 500 years ago, he introduced the civilized world to reliable accounting. Transactions were recorded twice (once to show where an item came from, and then to show where it went), so that nothing could be missed. Accountants today use the same principles – as well as following standards laid down by their own profession – to produce meaningful financial statements that summarize both the past and current financial position of an organization.

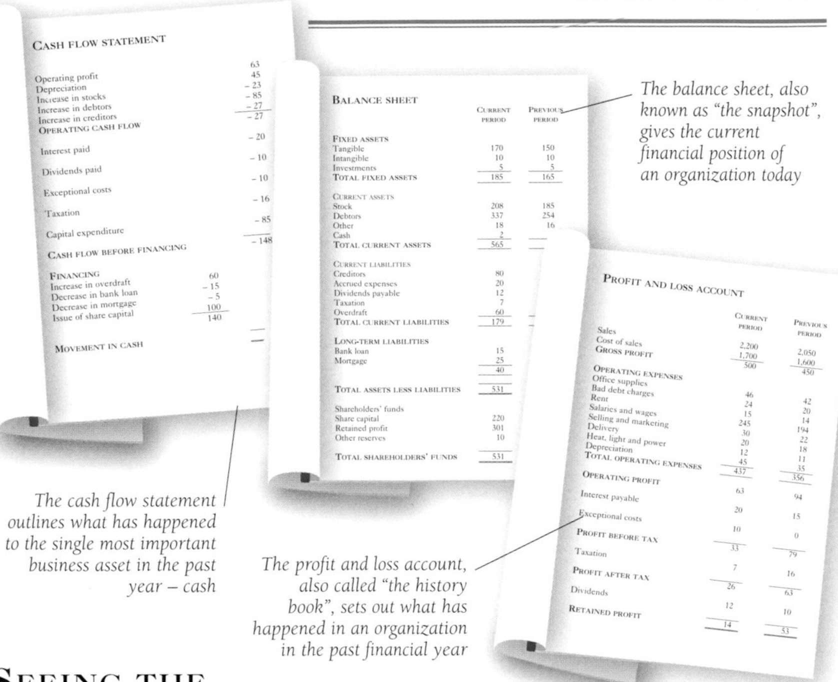

CASH FLOW STATEMENT

Operating profit		63
Depreciation		45
Increase in stocks		– 23
Increase in debtors		– 85
Increase in creditors		– 27
OPERATING CASH FLOW		– 27
Interest paid		– 20
Dividends paid		– 10
Exceptional costs		– 10
Taxation		– 16
Capital expenditure		– 85
CASH FLOW BEFORE FINANCING		– 148
FINANCING		
Increase in overdraft	60	
Decrease in bank loan	– 15	
Decrease in mortgage	– 5	
Issue of share capital	100	
	140	
MOVEMENT IN CASH		

BALANCE SHEET

	CURRENT PERIOD	PREVIOUS PERIOD
FIXED ASSETS		
Tangible	170	150
Intangible	10	10
Investments	5	5
TOTAL FIXED ASSETS	185	165
CURRENT ASSETS		
Stock	208	185
Debtors	337	254
Other	18	16
Cash	2	
TOTAL CURRENT ASSETS	565	
CURRENT LIABILITIES		
Creditors	80	
Accrued expenses	20	
Dividends payable	12	
Taxation	7	
Overdraft	60	
TOTAL CURRENT LIABILITIES	179	
LONG-TERM LIABILITIES		
Bank loan	15	
Mortgage	25	
	40	
TOTAL ASSETS LESS LIABILITIES	531	
Shareholders' funds		
Share capital	220	
Retained profit	301	
Other reserves	10	
TOTAL SHAREHOLDERS' FUNDS	531	

PROFIT AND LOSS ACCOUNT

	CURRENT PERIOD	PREVIOUS PERIOD
Sales	2,200	2,050
Cost of sales	1,700	1,600
GROSS PROFIT	500	450
OPERATING EXPENSES		
Office supplies	46	42
Bad debt charges	24	20
Rent	15	14
Salaries and wages	245	194
Selling and marketing	30	22
Delivery	20	18
Heat, light and power	12	11
Depreciation	45	35
TOTAL OPERATING EXPENSES	437	356
OPERATING PROFIT	63	94
Interest payable	20	15
Exceptional costs	10	0
PROFIT BEFORE TAX	33	79
Taxation	7	16
PROFIT AFTER TAX	26	63
Dividends	12	10
RETAINED PROFIT	14	53

The cash flow statement outlines what has happened to the single most important business asset in the past year – cash

The balance sheet, also known as "the snapshot", gives the current financial position of an organization today

The profit and loss account, also called "the history book", sets out what has happened in an organization in the past financial year

SEEING THE TRUE PICTURE

Each time you examine the financial statements that make up a set of business accounts, keep some key points in mind. First, since all businesses have different accounting policies and adding-up methods, no two sets of accounts will be the same. Second, different business formats (partnerships or limited liability companies, for example) and types (such as manufacturing or service organizations) will operate in different ways, with the result that some accounts are straightforward and others complex. Accounts may also be produced for a variety of reasons, such as calculating tax liability, assessing investment potential, or establishing a value for sale. Remember this when you interpret the figures.

▲ IDENTIFYING THE KEY FINANCIAL STATEMENTS

There are three financial statements that will help you assess the success of a company. Broadly, the profit and loss account reveals the income less expenses, the balance sheet shows the assets less the liabilities, and the cash flow statement records the increase or decrease of cash.

3 Understand that accounts do no more than reflect financial reality.

WHO USES ACCOUNTS?

Accounts are of interest to everyone associated with the organization that produces them and to outsiders such as competitors and tax authorities. Add to your understanding of accounts by learning how to look at them from different points of view.

4 Recognize that accounts are produced for different purposes.

5 Be clear on why it is vital to examine your company's accounts.

WHO NEEDS ACCOUNTS?

There are two main groups of people who use accounts: those who are interested in the financial performance of an organization (such as investors, shareholders, lenders, or suppliers), and those who take a broader view (often for taxation, regulatory, or legal reasons). The latter are more interested in general issues such as compliance with appropriate legislation than in the detailed financial analysis.

DEFINING PERSPECTIVES

In addition to annual reports and accounts for external consumption, most organizations produce internal, or management, accounts. These are used only within the organization and are helpfully flexible in measuring different (sometimes non-financial) aspects of performance because they are not subject to the rules and regulations that govern the preparation of external figures. However, because internal accounts do not have to adhere to any rules, they often bear little or no resemblance to annual external accounts. The internals can simply be wrong, causing problems for managers who are using them to drive the business forward.

Manager wants to know where performance can be improved

INTERNAL ACCOUNTS

Tax official checks that correct tax has been paid on profits

EXTERNAL ACCOUNTS

LOOKING AT DIFFERENT ACCOUNTS ▶

External accounts show consistency and comparability. Internal accounts need not follow any rules and can be more flexible and useful to a business, but also more open to error.

IDENTIFYING USERS OF ACCOUNTS

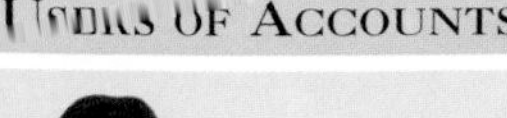

USERS OF ACCOUNTS	WHAT THEY LOOK FOR
OWNER Has a vested interest in the organization's future and success; tends to be financially cautious.	• How well the business is doing compared with previous years and with competitors. • Reassurance that the family source of income is safe and secure.
 **INVESTOR/SHAREHOLDER** Invests money or has shares in an organization; their analysis is often detailed and ruthless.	• Information on an organization to allow comparisons with other businesses, with a view to choosing between them. • Indications that returns will be maximized.
 **LENDER** Advances loans; needs to know that the interest is affordable and that the debt can be repaid.	• Evidence that an organization will be able to pay the interest on any debts. • The worth of an organization should the debt be unpaid and the business wound up.
 **COMPETITOR** Has an interest in the relative financial performance and business statistics of rivals.	• Growth in sales, market share, net profits, and overall business efficiency. • Information about the cost structure and operations of competitors.
 **MANAGER/EMPLOYEE** Works for and is paid by the organization on a full-time or regular basis.	• Reassurance that the organization will continue to operate competitively. • End-of-year figures that reflect his/her competence favourably.
 **CUSTOMER/SUPPLIER** Needs to know whether he/she is dealing with financially sound and reputable organizations.	• Continuity of supply and business without disruption to the flow of goods or services. • Ability of an organization to pay for goods and deliver on time.
 **TAXATION OFFICIAL** Reviews financial statements for accuracy and reasonableness, then checks the amount of tax payable.	• Properly prepared and computed accounts and profit and loss statements. • Validity of accounts when compared with similar businesses.

EXAMINING REGULATIONS AND PRACTICE

The drawing up of accounts is governed both by strict legal requirements and by more informal guidelines created by the accounting profession. Understand the principles and the influences that have shaped the way in which accounts are prepared.

6 Understand the impact of the law and the accounting profession.

7 Accept that minimal information is usually disclosed.

8 Keep up to date with accounting methods.

FOLLOWING THE LAW

In most countries the primary rules for producing accounts are laid down by law. This states exactly what must be done in creating, managing, and closing down a company – in short, the law establishes the overall framework, or "skeleton", for producing accounts. While the law is usually clear on the "what" and "when" of accounts, it is often vague on such issues as "how should stock be valued?" or "how should profit be recognized on a particular transaction?". This detailed, practical level of accounting is usually left to accountants.

ASSESSING GUIDELINES

For those accounting issues where the law gives insufficient guidance, accountants have established their own set of guidelines and standards known as Generally Accepted Accounting Principles (GAAP). Country-specific, GAAP advises how certain key transactions are best treated. Because GAAP is not compulsory, compliance with it may be less than perfect, which is why abuse of the system is possible. Additional rules may also apply to certain businesses, depending on company size, ownership, and listing rules of stock exchanges.

QUESTIONS TO ASK YOURSELF

Q What size of business am I looking at, and what level and detail of accounting disclosure should I expect to see?

Q What does the law require the accounts to contain, and how informative will I find this?

Q Are the accounting policies of the organization typical and reasonable for a business of its size and type?

COMPARING PRACTICE IN DIFFERENT COUNTRIES

The rules governing the preparation and structure of accounts are unusual. Strict legal requirements laid down by a country's law, together with generally accepted but more informal practice typically created by the accounting profession of that country, may be either strong or weak, depending on the country. Countries with strong "codified" law and tax regimes (Continental Europe in general) tend to have weaker GAAP, and vice versa. Strong and open stock exchanges typically have strong GAAP, since, unlike laws, GAAP guidelines can be drawn up relatively quickly in response to real-life issues.

CHOOSING POLICIES

Operating within both the law and GAAP, organizations choose how they will treat certain financial transactions. Known as accounting policies, these are generally selected by the directors of an organization and their business advisers as being the most appropriate to the company's current circumstances and also the best way of fairly presenting their results and financial position. Since no two organizations are the same, they will obviously all add up their accounts in a slightly different way.

9 Realize that adding-up methods vary around the world.

▼ DEFINING INFLUENCES ON ACCOUNTS

Of the five key influences on accounting statements, company law and accounting practice have most impact on the form that accounts take, followed by regulatory and taxation bodies, and international rules.

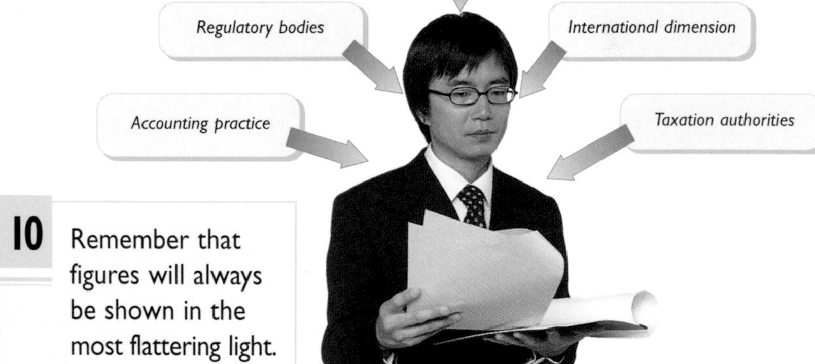

10 Remember that figures will always be shown in the most flattering light.

DEFINING KEY CONCEPTS

There are certain fundamental themes or concepts, such as accruals, prudence, consistency, and viability, that are seen as the cornerstones of good accounting. In order to understand accounts it is vital to appreciate the importance of these.

11 Commit the four basic accounting principles to memory.

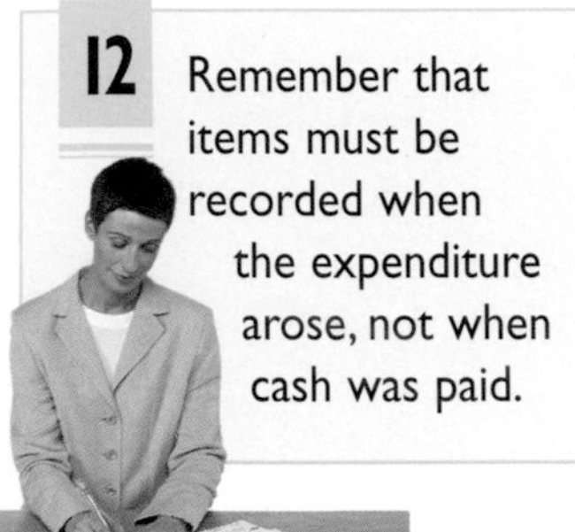

12 Remember that items must be recorded when the expenditure arose, not when cash was paid.

USING ACCRUALS

The principle of accruals, or matching, sets out when a transaction should appear in the accounts. An item is always recorded when the income (or expenditure) arises – not when cash is received (or paid). For example, even when a sale is made on credit terms and cash may not be received until the next accounting period, the sale must still be recognized now. While applying this fundamental accounting principle is commonsense, it neverthless causes most accounting problems.

SHOWING PRUDENCE AND CONSISTENCY

Financial statements must be prudently or conservatively presented, which means that profits must not be overstated, and costs must be realistically and fairly estimated. In other words, figures should be on the pessimistic side. Prudence addresses the question: "how much should an amount be?" and is the most important of the key concepts. Accounts should also be produced using consistent assumptions and treatments. This means that an organization should use similar principles year-on-year, so that accounts can be compared sensibly. Changes to assumptions and treatments can, of course, be made but the financial implications must be highlighted and quantified.

POINTS TO REMEMBER

- The accruals principle asks the question: "in which accounting period" or "when" should the impact of a transaction be shown?
- Prudence, or financial conservatism, effectively overrides all other accounting principles in importance.

13 Know that prudence governs fair accounting.

ASSUMING VIABILITY

When producing a set of accounts it is necessary to assume that the organization will be in business, or a going concern, the following year. This is a silent assumption, since it would be almost impossible to produce accounts if the business were likely to fail. The value of stock in a warehouse, a plant, a piece of equipment, or any other item in the accounts would be affected if the business were to cease to exist.

14 Be aware that any change in adding up often indicates something to hide.

EXPLAINING KEY TERMS

KEY TERM	DEFINITION
ASSET	Anything owned by an organization that has a monetary value, from plant and machinery to patents and goodwill.
AUDIT	Independent inspection of accounts, according to set principles, by accountants who are qualified auditors.
DEPRECIATION	Annual cost shown in the profit and loss account of writing off a fixed asset over its expected useful life.
EQUITY	Share capital and reserves of a company, which represent what shareholders have invested in the organization.
FIXED ASSET	Asset used in a business and not held for resale, typically with a life of more than one year.
LIABILITY	Amount owed at a set time, often split into short term (less than one year) and long term (more than one year).
RESERVES	Profits made by a business, which have been invested in the business rather than paid out in dividends.
WORKING CAPITAL	Capital available for daily operations of an organization, usually expressed as current assets less current liabilities.

MASTERING ACCOUNTS

Mastering accounts means understanding the three key financial statements: the profit and loss account, the balance sheet, and the cash flow statement. Learn how they all fit together.

UNDERSTANDING A PROFIT AND LOSS ACCOUNT

The profit and loss account is an organization's statement of earnings; it shows all the income less expenses over the year. Make sure that you know how the profit and loss account is structured and what type of items are included.

15 Check how the accounting policies show that profit is measured.

RECORDING THE PAST

The profit and loss account is a "history book" of the past year. It tells how well a business has performed, listing all the "ins less outs", or sales less costs. Working on the accruals principle, only items arising during the year are shown. They must also be of a "revenue" nature (goods, services, and general annual expenditure), never items of a "capital" nature (purchase or sale of fixed assets such as equipment and machinery).

16 Remember only "revenue" items appear in a profit and loss account.

READING THE LINES

A profit and loss account measures various levels, or "lines", of profit. First is gross profit: sales (sometimes called gross income or fees billed) less cost of sales (the costs of providing goods or services). Next is operating profit: gross profit less all the expenses supporting the infrastructure and administration of an organization. Profit before tax is the operating profit less interest incurred on borrowings for the year, plus interest received. Profit after tax is calculated by deducting the tax due as a result of trading for the year. Retained profit is the after-tax profit less any dividend paid to the shareholders.

PROFIT AND LOSS ACCOUNT

	CURRENT PERIOD	PREVIOUS PERIOD
Sales	2,200	2,050
Cost of sales	1,700	1,600
GROSS PROFIT	500	450
OPERATING EXPENSES		
Office supplies	46	42
Bad debt charges	24	20
Rent	15	14
Salaries and wages	245	194
Selling and marketing	30	22
Delivery	20	18
Heat, light and power	12	11
Depreciation	45	35
TOTAL OPERATING EXPENSES	437	356
OPERATING PROFIT	63	94
Interest payable	20	15
Exceptional costs	10	0
PROFIT BEFORE TAX	33	79
Taxation	7	16
PROFIT AFTER TAX	26	63
Dividends	12	10
RETAINED PROFIT	14	53

▲ **RECOGNIZING THE FORMAT**

A typical profit and loss account is consistently structured into set rows and columns to show the profit or loss for the year; that is, the difference between income and expenditure.

DECIDING WHAT COUNTS

Items included in the profit and loss account must all have passed the accruals test, but there are times when deciding what should be counted as sales or expenses is tricky. For example, should a sales invoice be included in the accounts if the work has not been completed? Accountants use various signposts to help them recognize what and how much to include, and when to do so. These signposts include the following:

- Completion: is the work substantially completed?
- Ownership: has ownership passed from the vendor to the customer?
- Measurement: can the profit be accurately and prudently estimated?
- Irrevocability: could the customer cancel the sale, causing the loss of profit?

17 Understand what the main headings in a profit and loss account mean.

LOOKING AT GROSS PROFIT

The gross profit, or first line of profit, provides an important early measure of a business's wellbeing. Ensure that you understand which type of expenses are deducted to calculate gross profit and what the gross margin can tell you.

18 Remember that the gross profit percentage should not be falling.

19 Compare your company's accounts year-on-year and with competitors'.

20 Be aware that gross profit measures a company's basic viability.

RECORDING SALES

The first item on a profit and loss account records a business's overall volume of activity and is called either sales, turnover, income, or fees billed. This is the full amount of all the sales invoices raised during the accounting period that have met the correct accruals criteria for being included on the statement. These are stated less any sales-related taxes (since tax belongs to the Internal Revenue Service, not the organization itself).

▼ DETECTING GROSS PROFIT

The first three lines of a profit and loss account show an organization's fundamental financial performance in black and white. From it, the wellbeing of the business can be determined.

PROFIT AND LOSS ACCOUNT

	CURRENT PERIOD	PREVIOUS PERIOD
Sales	2,200	2,050
Cost of sales	1,700	1,600
GROSS PROFIT	500	450
OPERATING EXPENSES		
Office supplies	46	42
Bad debt charges	24	20
Rent	15	14
	245	194

The previous period's figures are shown so that they can be easily compared with this period's results

Gross profit is the key result of a business and the first figure that investors or owners are likely to be interested in

DEDUCTING COST OF SALES

There are two types of costs in the profit and loss account and these are deducted separately. The first group is known as cost of sales (COS), sometimes referred to as cost of goods sold (COGS). These are all the costs expended to make or produce the product or service that is being sold, and usually include materials, production staff, production premises, and machinery costs – typically "factory" costs.

POINTS TO REMEMBER

- Gross profit percentage may well vary between businesses.
- The "busy fool syndrome" is where a business may be increasing its sales but making little profit from them.
- Gross margin percentage is the most useful comparison tool between businesses.

21 Look beyond the figures to the type and structure of the organization.

PROVIDING A MEASURE

While gross income, or the full amount of sales, is an important sign of life for a business, gross profit, or the full amount of sales less COS, is more informative about its health. This "factory result" is often more usefully expressed as a percentage of sales. Since different businesses have different COS, they will have different gross profit percentages. These must be looked at in relation to what would be expected from the type of business.

PERFECT PRINTERS
PROFIT AND LOSS ACCOUNT

	CURRENT PERIOD	%	PREVIOUS PERIOD	%
Sales	2,200	100.0	2,050	100.0
Cost of sales	600	27.3	560	27.3
GROSS PROFIT	1,600	72.7	1,490	72.7
OPERATING EXPENSES				
Office supplies	46	2.1		

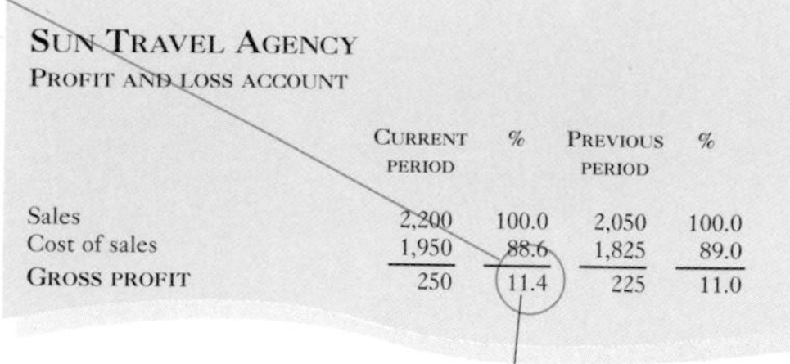

SUN TRAVEL AGENCY
PROFIT AND LOSS ACCOUNT

	CURRENT PERIOD	%	PREVIOUS PERIOD	%
Sales	2,200	100.0	2,050	100.0
Cost of sales	1,950	88.6	1,825	89.0
GROSS PROFIT	250	11.4	225	11.0

Profit margins for low cost of sales businesses are typically between 50 and 90 per cent; for high cost of sales businesses they rarely exceed 10 per cent

▲ COMPARING GROSS 'ROFIT MARGINS

;ross profit margins vary significantly etween different types of business, and a ›w margin is to be expected from a usiness with a high cost of sales, such as supermarket or travel agency. On the ther hand, a service business with a ›wer than normal cost of sales will have higher than average gross profit margin.

DETERMINING OPERATING PROFIT

The second line of profit is operating or trading profit, which is a clear measure of a business's performance after all its operating costs have been deducted. Identify which costs apply and so ascertain how successfully a business has been managed.

22 Examine operating costs to gauge management efficiency.

23 Look at trends in certain costs to anticipate any future problems.

DEDUCTING OTHER COSTS

The second type of costs in the profit and loss account, which are now deducted to determine operating profit, are called selling, general, and administration (SG&A) costs, or operating expenses. These cover any expenses not listed in the cost of sales category. SG&A includes marketing and advertising under "selling", while "general and administration" costs cover head office, accounting, information technology, marketing, personnel, directors, and central costs. All costs must be either COS or SG&A.

CALCULATING ▼ OPERATING PROFIT

Operating profit is struck after the remainder of costs in a business have been deducted. It is usually expressed as a percentage of sales.

Sales		
Cost of sales	1,700	1,600
GROSS PROFIT	500	450
OPERATING EXPENSES		
Office supplies	46	42
Bad debt charges	24	20
Rent	15	14
Salaries and wages	245	194
Selling and marketing	30	22
Delivery	20	18
Heat, light and power	12	11
Depreciation	45	35
TOTAL OPERATING EXPENSES	437	356
OPERATING PROFIT	63	94
Interest payable	20	15

Total operating expenses are deducted from the gross profit

Operating profit made from trading, before the deduction of taxes, interest, and dividends

UNDERSTANDING DIFFERENT CYCLES

All businesses have two cycles – an operating cycle and a capital investment cycle. The operating cycle is straightforward: a business buys goods or services in order that they can be sold on at a profit. The capital investment cycle, on the other hand, is a measure of how much is invested in the fabric of a business (such as the plant, tools, or machinery) in order that a business may carry out its operating cycle. More than one operating cycle is generally needed to fund one capital cycle. A set of accounts simply reflects how much money is tied up in an organization at any time in both these cycles.

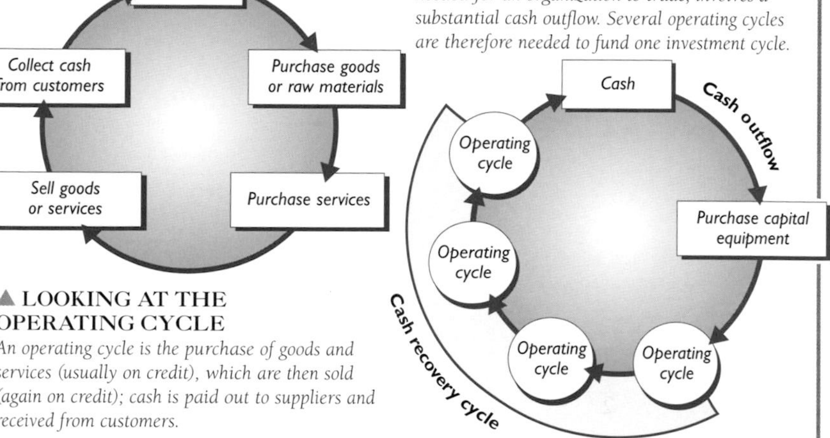

▼ **REVIEWING THE CAPITAL INVESTMENT CYCLE**

Capital investment, or the purchase of one-off items needed for an organization to trade, involves a substantial cash outflow. Several operating cycles are therefore needed to fund one investment cycle.

▲ **LOOKING AT THE OPERATING CYCLE**

An operating cycle is the purchase of goods and services (usually on credit), which are then sold (again on credit); cash is paid out to suppliers and received from customers.

ꞡEACHING A SUB-TOTAL

)educting SG&A costs from gross profit gives the ub-total of operating profit. This is effectively ıe end of the "first half" of the profit and loss ccount, which measures how well a business as performed in its core operations. Operating rofit is often more usefully expressed as a ercentage of sales – a typical range being etween zero and 10 per cent.

24

Compare operating profit percentages between organizations.

EVALUATING THE BOTTOM LINE

The second half of the profit and loss statement, down to the "bottom line", relates to other expenses, including taxation and interest. It is vital to learn how to interpret these items, since their financial impact can often be significant.

25 Determine whether an interest bill is really affordable.

26 Check if one-off costs are warning signs of problems.

LOOKING AT INTEREST

Below the operating profit the next deduction to be made is the amount of interest incurred on all loans and borrowings over the period covered by the profit and loss account. This is often an issue because the amount payable can call into question the viability of an entire business. Affordability can be calculated by comparing the interest charges for the year to the operating profit. For example, if operating profit is £63 and interest £20, the interest could be paid about three times over and interest cover is said to be "three". There is no absolute target; what is important is the trend in interest cover, which can change from year to year.

REACHING THE BOTTOM LINE ▼

The difference between operating profit and retained profit will be due to varying amounts of interest, exceptional items, taxation, and dividends.

TOTAL OPERATING EXPENSES		356
OPERATING PROFIT	63	94
Interest payable	20	15
Exceptional costs	10	0
PROFIT BEFORE TAX	33	79
Taxation	7	16
PROFIT AFTER TAX	26	63
Dividends	12	10
RETAINED PROFIT	14	53

Profit after tax is what is left for shareholders after interest, exceptional costs, and taxes have been deducted

After paying shareholders' dividends, the business reinvests the retained profit

EXAMINING EXCEPTIONAL COSTS

Occasionally you will come across other items of a one-off, non-recurring nature, and traditionally these are shown separately to the core gross and operating profit figures so as not to distort them. Such items are referred to as exceptional items and typically include provisions for large future events (recognizing costs now even though the event will happen in the future), currency movements, gains and losses on sales of assets or businesses, and pensions. Assess whether these seem reasonable, or if they indicate problems.

EXAMINING TAXATION

The operating profit minus interest gives profit before tax (PBT), which is subject to taxation; the profit and loss account details the tax bill on the year's profits. The amount is unlikely yet to have been paid in full to the Internal Revenue Service and is also probably a best estimate. Whatever the annual tax charge is computed to be, it is deducted from PBT to give profit after tax, or PAT, which, in principle, belongs to the shareholders. PAT also provides a basis for calculating shareholder measures such as earnings per share.

27 Investigate a tax bill if it is not the expected rate.

28 Spot the trend in, and sufficiency of, retained profits.

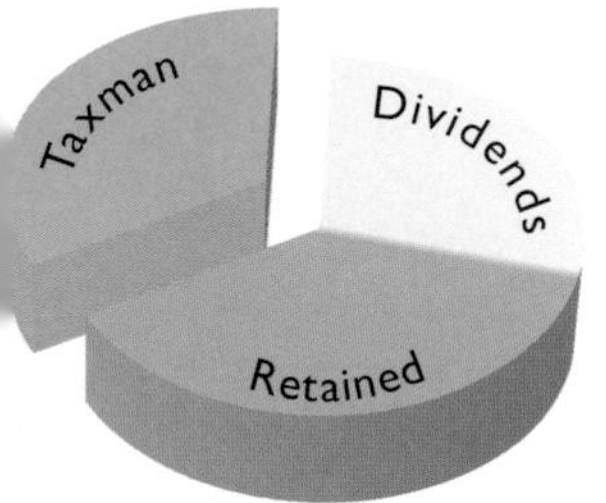

▲ SPLITTING PROFIT BEFORE TAX

For a quoted company, profit before tax is split three ways. One-third represents tax (where corporate tax rate is approximately 30%), one-third is typically paid to shareholders by way of dividend, and the final one-third is retained in the business.

PINPOINTING RETAINED PROFIT

At the bottom line of the profit and loss account, once declared dividends have been deducted, are retained earnings. These represent the profit kept behind by an organization in order to help it grow. Bear in mind that profits make a balance sheet grow, so the amount of retained profit should correspond to the increase in the balance sheet. However, in large companies this simple accounting truth may be obscured by technical shuffling. It may also be unclear exactly where the retained profit will be; it is hoped that it would be in cash form in a successful organization, rather than in a less liquid item, such as stock.

UNDERSTANDING BALANCE SHEETS

The balance sheet is effectively a listing of everything a business owns less all that it owes. Learn how this key financial statement is structured and how the figures work to provide you with a picture of the total net assets of an organization.

29 Think of the balance sheet as an aerial photograph.

BALANCE SHEET	CURRENT PERIOD	PREVIOUS PERIOD
FIXED ASSETS		
Tangible	170	150
Intangible	10	10
Investments	5	5
TOTAL FIXED ASSETS	185	165
CURRENT ASSETS		
Stock	208	185
Debtors	337	254
Other	18	16
Cash	2	10
TOTAL CURRENT ASSETS	565	465
CURRENT LIABILITIES		
Creditors	80	109
Accrued expenses	20	18
Dividends payable	12	10
Taxation	7	16
Overdraft	60	0
TOTAL CURRENT LIABILITIES	179	153
LONG-TERM LIABILITIES		
Bank loan	15	30
Mortgage	25	30
	40	60
TOTAL ASSETS LESS LIABILITIES	531	417
Shareholders' funds		
Share capital	220	120
Retained profit	301	287
Other reserves	10	10
TOTAL SHAREHOLDERS' FUNDS	531	417

▲ READING THE BALANCE SHEET

The balance sheet lists assets and liabilities comparing both previous and current accounting periods, grouping them into meaningful sub-totals and totals that explain what is happening financially within an organization.

EXAMINING HOW BALANCE SHEETS WORK

The balance sheet shows the present financial performance of a business. It can be compared to a snapshot of an entire organization taken at the close of business on a specific day, and it is therefore correct only at that one precise moment. The snapshot shows everything that the business owns – its assets – and all that it owes – its liabilities. Balance sheets are generally drawn up each year at the same time as the profit and loss account. But bear in mind that pictures can be flattering. If, for example, a fashion retailer's balance sheet is done after the summer sales (when there is plenty of cash in the bank and stocks are low), it will look particularly good.

QUESTIONS TO ASK YOURSELF

- **Q** Does the year-end fit the annual nature of the business?
- **Q** Would a different accounting date alter the balance sheet?
- **Q** Have there been major changes in any sums year-on-year?
- **Q** Have assets shown at current value been estimated fairly?

GROUPING FIGURES

The balance sheet is split into sections, according to strict accounting rules. The first section lists an organization's assets split between fixed (or long-term) and current (or short-term) assets. The second section itemizes liabilities (again split between fixed and current). The third shows shareholders' funds, or money invested in the business by its owners.

30 Understand the importance of how liabilities and assets are grouped.

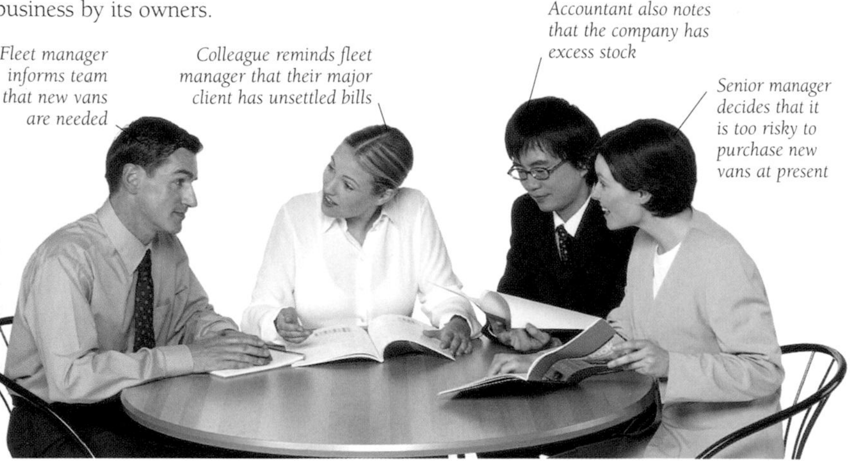

Fleet manager informs team that new vans are needed

Colleague reminds fleet manager that their major client has unsettled bills

Accountant also notes that the company has excess stock

Senior manager decides that it is too risky to purchase new vans at present

USING THE ▲ BALANCE SHEET

As a manager, it is important to look at, understand, and act upon what the balance sheet tells you. In this way you will be able to make better quality financial decisions.

31 Appreciate that balance sheets show cost and not value.

INTERPRETING THE TOTAL

All assets and liabilities are generally shown on the balance sheet according to an accounting convention called historic cost, which means that they are shown at their original cost to the business. The balance sheet total, also referred to as total net assets, is arrived at by adding up the cost of all assets and then deducting the total of short- and long-term liabilities. Remember that the balance sheet normally shows only costs, and it should not be seen as an indication of an organization's market value. Nothing could be further from the truth, yet it remains a popular misconception.

EXAMINING FIXED ASSETS

Fixed assets are used by a business on a permanent basis to create wealth in the normal course of operations. Learn to recognize the three types of fixed assets (tangibles, intangibles, and investments) and understand the concept of depreciation.

32 Investigate any significant additions in unusual fixed assets.

33 Scrutinize closely any asset that is shown at current value.

RECOGNIZING TANGIBLE FIXED ASSETS

Assets needed for a business to be in a position to trade are known as fixed assets. These are typically tangible items with a life of more than 12 months (otherwise they would be shown as a cost on the profit and loss). Spending on fixed assets is called capital expenditure, and this reflects how much is invested in the fabric of a business in order that it may carry out its operating cycle. Typical fixed assets are land, buildings, equipment, machinery, computers, fixtures and fittings, and vehicles. Manufacturers generally have high fixed assets and are capital-intensive. Service businesses have low fixed assets and are not capital-intensive.

UNDERSTANDING ▼ FIXED ASSETS

Fixed assets are generally grouped into tangible, intangible, and investments held for the longer term. They are listed in order of the frequency in which they are encountered. Amounts are stated after depreciation.

BALANCE SHEET	CURRENT PERIOD	PREVIOUS PERIOD
FIXED ASSETS		
Tangible	170	150
Intangible	10	10
Investments	5	5
TOTAL FIXED ASSETS	185	165
CURRENT ASSETS		
Stock	208	185
Debtors	337	254
Other	18	16
Cash	2	10
TOTAL CURRENT ASSETS	565	465

Total fixed assets shows how much is invested in a business to enable it to trade

ANALYZING DEPRECIATION

Fixed assets are shown at cost less depreciation, known as net book value. Depreciation writes off the cost of the asset (less any anticipated residual value, often assumed to be nil) over its effective useful life. For example, assuming a computer costs £900 and has a useful life of three years, it will be depreciated by £300 a year. This means that it will be written down to £600 after one year, £300 after two years, and £0 after three years. Depreciation simply spreads the cost of a fixed asset over its lifetime; it does not write the asset down to secondhand value, nor does it provide a fund of money for replacement.

▼ CALCULATING DEPRECIATION

With the "straight line" method, a computer would be written off by an equal annual amount throughout its depreciable life. Using the "reducing balance" method, the depreciation of a car would be recalculated every year based on the net book value (or written down value) reached to date.

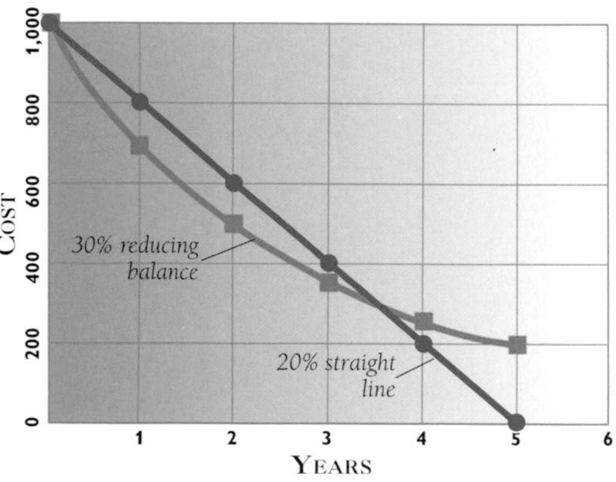

34 See that an asset's life and depreciation rate seem fair.

FLYING ON TIME ▼

The useful economic life of an asset is usually written off over a number of years. With an aircraft, however, the number of hours flown is considered to be a far better determinant of age.

SETTING A RATE

The depreciation life/rate of each asset is set by the business, so although different companies are making the same trading profit, because their fixed assets have different depreciation lives, each will show a different accounting profit. In addition to the straight line on cost and reducing balance methods of depreciating an asset, there are any number of other ways to depreciate assets, most of which are simply based on commonsense and generally accepted practice.

DEFINING INTANGIBLES

Most fixed assets are real and tangible; in other words, they physically exist and can be touched. Yet balance sheets recognize that certain long-term assets may not be tangible. There are two main types of intangibles: traditional and modern. Traditional intangibles include items such as patents, intellectual property rights, and know-how, while modern intangibles (or those that have recently become popular) are goodwill and brands. Intangibles, by their very nature, are often difficult to value, but – like all fixed assets – once their worth has been calculated, they must be depreciated over their useful economic life.

POINTS TO REMEMBER

- Certain intangibles have been shown in accounts for many years without creating problems.
- Goodwill is no more than an amount needed to get the figures to balance; it might also represent something intangible of value.
- Including the value of brands in a balance sheet involves much subjectivity and can often be very controversial.

35 See if intangibles make up a realistic proportion of the balance sheet.

EXPLAINING GOODWILL

Goodwill is generally taken to mean the value of a business's good name, reputation, and client base. Goodwill is shown as a fixed asset by an organization when it buys another business at a higher price than the value of its assets. Any decent business will be worth more than simply its assets, but the problem is how to get the accounts of the buyer to balance. When buying a business for £10 that has assets of only £6, the difference of £4 is called goodwill. Goodwill is shown as an intangible asset and is amortized (depreciated) over its useful economic life.

Purchase price is established by mutual agreement

NOTES TO ACCOUNTS

COMPANY	A	B	C
Amount paid for company	155	15	23
Fair value of acquired assets	95	2	-2
Goodwill	60	13	25

Amount of goodwill depends on the purchaser's perception of worth

Purchaser is so keen that it pays money to acquire liabilities

◀ **BALANCING THE BOOKS**
This extract from the notes to accounts shows an organization that has bought three companies during the year. The purchase price reflects the value of the acquired company as a whole, not just its assets. The amount of goodwill is simply the difference between the purchase price and the fair value of the assets acquired.

UNDERSTANDING BRANDS

A new development has seen the concept of goodwill taken even further, which is known as brand accounting. The idea is that because some organizations do not want to show a cost to the profit and loss account every year when depreciating goodwill (either because their profits will not stand it or because they do not believe that the asset in question should be written down), they categorize the asset as a "brand" rather than as goodwill. They argue that any spending on marketing and advertising means that the brand does not fall in value – and so is not being depreciated.

36 Check whether any brands should have been reduced in value.

CASE STUDY

Peter, the sales manager of a confectionery company, was disappointed that profits were down in spite of increased sales. In the latest set of accounts, Peter discovered that large amortization (depreciation) charges had been made because his company had acquired two businesses. Since the assets of the new businesses had been bought for more than their book value, the shortfall had been categorized as goodwill, which had to be written off over its useful life. As a result, profits were being reduced by the amount of the annual write-off. Peter approached David, the finance manager, to suggest that since so much money was being spent on marketing and advertising (expenditure in support of the brands), the goodwill should be classified as a brand. David agreed, and profits increased again.

▲ **AVOIDING DEPRECIATION CHARGES**

Peter's understanding of the issues of goodwill and brands prompted him to approach the finance manager with a sound proposition. By classifying goodwill as a brand, David was able to amend the company's accounts so that there was no annual write-off. As a result, Peter was happy to see his team's improved sales performance clearly reflected in the increased profit shown on the next period's profit and loss account.

EXPLORING INVESTMENTS

The final category of fixed assets is called investments, which covers any monies or shares held outside the company. These may be shares in another organization held for the long term, investments, or any other asset that will be sold, but not within the next 12 months. Again, the issue is that of cost. For example, should shares be valued at the price originally paid for them or according to the stock market price for that day? It is generally agreed that they should be shown at market value.

QUESTIONS TO ASK YOURSELF

Q Are all fixed assets fairly stated in cost and depreciation?

Q Do the figures demonstrate adequate investment for the future?

Q Should any intangibles be ignored when analyzing figures?

Q Have investments been valued and accounted for correctly?

WORKING WITH CURRENT ASSETS

Current assets are short-term assets that a business holds that will convert into cash within the next 12 months. Learn to recognize the four main types of current assets and why it is important to convert the first three into cash quickly.

37 Look at current assets with care; they represent a business's lifeblood.

38 Check that debtors change only in proportion to turnover.

LISTING CURRENT ASSETS

Included under current assets is cash, plus anything that will turn into cash in the next 12 months. The importance of current assets is that they show how much an organization has in the way of cash, or near cash, and therefore how viable the business is. There are three main categories of current assets: stock; debtors (people who have bought goods and owe payment); and other current assets, which include other monies owed and items known as prepayments. There is also cash (received when debtors pay their bills, and including petty cash or monies held in the business bank account or on short-term deposit)

UNDERSTANDING ▼ CURRENT ASSETS

Current assets, or items that will turn into cash in the next year, include stocks held for resale, debtors owing for credit sales made, sundry items paid for in advance, and cash itself.

TOTAL FIXED ASSETS	185	165
CURRENT ASSETS		
Stock	208	185
Debtors	337	254
Other	18	16
Cash	2	10
TOTAL CURRENT ASSETS	565	465
CURRENT LIABILITIES		
Creditors	80	109
Accrued expenses	20	18

Current assets in a business should be as "liquid" (close to cash) as possible

DEFINING STOCK

There are three components of stock: raw materials, work in progress, and finished goods. What is of interest is how much cash is tied up in each component, because the more raw materials there are, the further they must go to be converted into cash, incurring costs along the way. Finished goods are safer assets because they are more liquid. However, stock overall is the least liquid of all current assets.

LOOKING AT ASSETS WITHIN THE OPERATING CYCLE

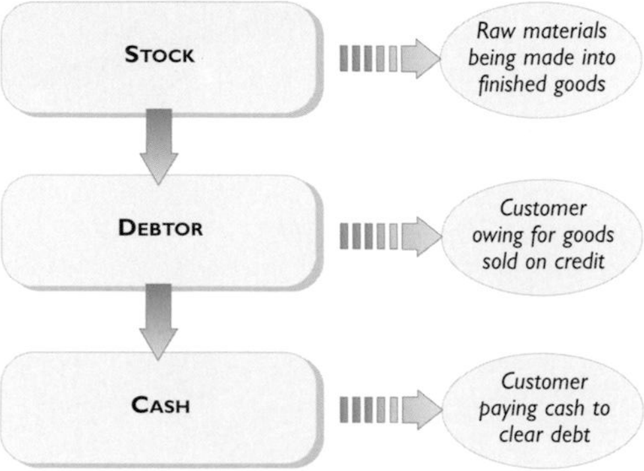

STOCK → *Raw materials being made into finished goods*

↓

DEBTOR → *Customer owing for goods sold on credit*

↓

CASH → *Customer paying cash to clear debt*

VALUING STOCK

Stock is usually valued either at cost or at net realizable value (whichever is lower), since stock should never be overstated. Cost is the price paid for the items when bought; realizable is what they could be sold for, net of expenses. An item bought for £5 with a selling price of £20 should be shown in stock at £5. If it could be sold for only £1, then that is how it should be shown, with a stock write-down of £4 (£5 minus £1) appearing as a cost of sales in that year's profit and loss account. The higher the stock at the end of the year (closing stock), the lower the cost of sales on the profit and loss account, hence the higher the reported profit.

39 Appreciate how stock on the balance sheet impacts profit on the profit and loss account.

DO'S AND DON'TS

- ✔ Do look for unexpected increases in stocks and debtors.
- ✔ Do be cynical about the valuation applied to stocks.
- ✗ Don't believe that more current assets are always good news.
- ✗ Don't overlook other current assets and what they tell you.

40 Realize that slow-moving and obsolete stock is a common problem.

IDENTIFYING STOCK

Assuming that prices of stock are rising, then raw materials purchased earlier will cost less than those bought later. Accountants generally choose one of two methods of charging a material out of the stores and on to the job: FIFO (first in, first out) or LIFO (last in, first out). The method chosen will affect reported profits and assets, since under FIFO the profit and loss account profit and balance sheet closing stock figures will be higher. Under LIFO, both figures will be lower.

41 Check that your own stock has not been overvalued; reject amounts that do not seem right.

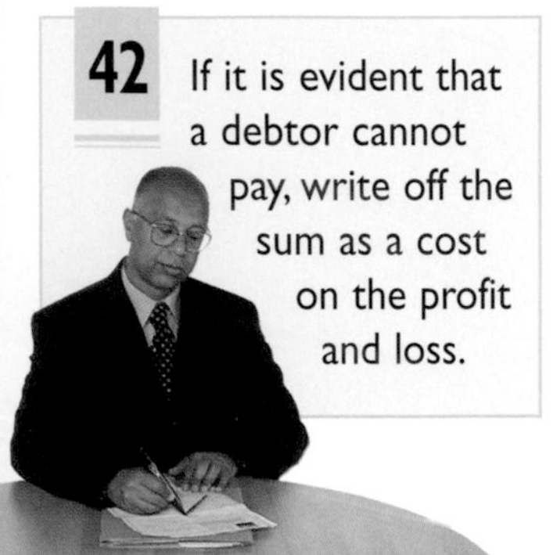

42 If it is evident that a debtor cannot pay, write off the sum as a cost on the profit and loss.

EXAMINING DEBTORS

Debtors, or amounts owed by customers for sales made on credit terms, is a more liquid asset than stock. The amount shown is the total of the invoices outstanding (issued but not yet paid) at the accounting period end, and it represents cash that is being held, albeit temporarily, by customers. Debtors will invariably be an organization's largest current asset – in which case it is vital that a business has them under control. This means making sure that customers pay, preferably on time and the full amount.

DEFINING DEDUCTIONS FROM DEBTORS

The problem with debtors is that not all of an organization's customers will end up paying – some may well default on the debt. Since accountants must follow the prudence principle and state all assets at a realistic figure, they must anticipate that a certain amount of debt will not be paid, and make a provision for it. This bad debt provision, which is estimated at the end of the year, is deducted from the debtors figure shown on the balance sheet. The difference between this year's and the previous year's provision then becomes a selling, general, and administration cost on the profit and loss account. Bad debts also impact on accounts during the year if, at any time, customers are unable to pay what they owe. Once this is apparent, their debt should be immediately cancelled. This is called a bad debt charge or write off, and is also an SG&A cost on the profit and loss account.

IDENTIFYING OTHER CURRENT ASSETS

CURRENT ASSET	POINTS TO NOTE
ASSETS HELD FOR RESALE Items about to be sold.	When a fixed asset such as land is about to be sold, it is shown on the balance sheet as a current asset, rather than as a fixed asset, because it will convert into cash within one year.
LOANS Advances to employees.	When an organization has lent or advanced money to its employees or directors, this is shown as a current asset of the business, since generally the monies will be fully repaid within the next year.
PREPAYMENTS Payments made in advance.	If bills are paid in advance, cash has been paid out – but the expense relates to a future accounting period. This means that a prepayment is, in effect, a current asset.
OTHERS Sundry items.	Insurance claims, tax refunds, deposits paid to secure goods, payments received by instalments, and stage payments represent sums owed that should be received within one year, hence they are current assets.

LISTING OTHER ITEMS

There are other items listed under current assets that can also be significant. Again the principle is that these will convert into cash within the next 12 months. Other assets typically include monies owed by people other than customers (such as a tax rebate that is due), and items that have been paid for in advance (such as rent or business rates), which could theoretically be reimbursed.

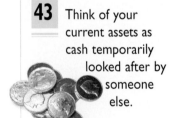

43 Think of your current assets as cash temporarily looked after by someone else.

44 Examine in detail the movement in cash for the period in question.

CLASSIFYING CASH

The most liquid of all current assets is cash – either at the bank or in hand. Cash includes everything that is a liquid asset, ranging from money in a bank account to cash in shop tills and petty cash tins throughout an organization. Money in a term deposit or with limited access rights is not strictly cash, so is listed under other current assets.

UNDERSTANDING LIABILITIES

Liabilities are debts payable in a future period because of events that have already happened. They are either current (due in the next 12 months) or long term. Learn to identify both types of liability and why the split between the two is important.

45 Check that an organization's liabilities do not exceed its assets.

46 Make sure that all possible liabilities have been included.

EXAMINING CURRENT LIABILITIES

Typical current liabilities are large items such as creditors (people who are owed money for goods purchased) and bank overdrafts (always repayable on demand). A business does not want what it owes (current liabilities) to exceed what it has coming in (current assets), since this is a recipe for insolvency. However, an enterprise that uses its creditors as a source of funding from a position of strength is not a cause for concern; if it cannot afford to pay its creditors, that is a sign of trouble.

SPLITTING LIABILITIES ▼

Liabilities are split into immediate and future obligations. On some balance sheets, current liabilities are deducted from current assets to give a net current assets subtotal. Then long-term liabilities are shown.

Cash		
TOTAL CURRENT ASSETS	565	465
CURRENT LIABILITIES		
Creditors	80	109
Accrued expenses	20	18
Dividends payable	12	10
Taxation	7	16
Overdraft	60	0
TOTAL CURRENT LIABILITIES	179	153
LONG-TERM LIABILITIES		
Bank loan	15	30
Mortgage	25	30
	40	60
TOTAL ASSETS LESS LIABILITIES	531	417

Current liabilities are typically listed in order of liquidity

Deducting current and long-term liabilities from total current assets gives the balance sheet total

IDENTIFYING OTHER CURRENT LIABILITIES

LIABILITY	POINTS TO NOTE
CREDITORS Sums owed to suppliers for purchases.	Some purchases of goods or services used during the year may not have been paid for; amounts owed to suppliers are shown as creditors, which are usually due within the next 12 months.
TAXATION Amounts owed to tax authorities.	Tax on profits, tax on capital gains, and other taxes may not have been paid in full – especially if not legally required to be paid until later. Outstanding amounts are shown as current liabilities.
DIVIDENDS Monies payable to shareholders.	Dividends are typically paid twice a year, with the second (or final) dividend declared but not yet paid. This is a current liability since it will inevitably be payable within the next 12 months.
LEASING Sums owed to leasing and hire purchase companies.	Amounts shown in current liabilities are only those that must be paid to the leasing or hire purchase company within 12 months. Instalments due after that year are long-term liabilities.
ACCRUALS Payments owed to providers of goods and services.	General bills (such as for telephones and electricity), accounting fees, auditing costs, and so on will have been incurred but not yet paid for. These are all shown under the general title of accruals.
SHORT-TERM DEBT Sums payable to a bank or providers of finance.	A bank overdraft is a current liability, since it is strictly repayable on demand. A repayment towards long-term debt that must be made in the next 12 months is also a current liability.

RECOGNIZING LONG-TERM LIABILITIES

Amounts payable by a business more than one year from the balance sheet date are long-term liabilities. These are items such as long-term debts and loans, mortgages, and formalized borrowing instruments such as debentures. They may be more technical, as in the case of provisions, which are taken out of this year's profits to pay for something in a future period. The point of splitting liabilities into current and long-term groups is to see how comfortably the business can repay its immediate debt.

POINTS TO REMEMBER

- Liabilities are amounts owed by an organization because of transactions that have already taken place.
- In time, all long-term liabilities will become short-term liabilities, which will, in turn, have to be paid off.
- Any increase in debt should be for a good reason, whether to increase trading volumes or to acquire fixed assets.

ANALYZING SHAREHOLDERS' FUNDS

This part of the balance sheet shows the funds put into or left in an organization by its shareholders. It must therefore equal the total net assets, or balance sheet total. It is here that you can learn where the money invested in the balance sheet has come from.

47 Remember that the funds of shareholders are always at risk.

48 Look at retained reserves to discover past profitability.

LOOKING AT SHARE CAPITAL

Share capital is essentially the money that shareholders have put into the business, for no guaranteed return or guaranteed payment. If a company raises, say, £1 million of share capital, the share capital account and the bank account both increase by £1 million – all nicely in balance.

UNDERSTANDING RETAINED PROFIT

The second major source of shareholders' funds is retained profit. Calculated from the profit and loss account, this is essentially the cumulative retained profit made each year since the company started. Retained profit is usually the most important source (in terms of size) of continued funding of a business.

▼ **CALCULATING SHAREHOLDERS' FUNDS**

This part of the balance sheet looks at where the money has come from in a business and will typically consist of share capital, retained profit, and technical reserves.

Shareholders' funds		
Share capital	220	120
Retained profit	301	287
Technical reserves	10	10
TOTAL SHAREHOLDERS' FUNDS	531	417

The total equity and reserves must equal the balance sheet total of assets less liabilities

DEFINING TECHNICAL RESERVES

There are other items shown in this part of the balance sheet that are known as technical reserves. Two types that appear most frequently are share premium and revaluation reserve. A share premium is the result of a company selling shares for a higher price than their nominal value. For example, if a £1 share is sold for £5, then it has been sold at a premium of £4. This share premium is not strictly retained profit, because it has not been made in the course of trading, so it has to be shown separately under technical reserves. A revaluation reserve occurs when an organization revalues an asset (such as a property) to show its current value rather than its original cost. Again, this is not strictly retained profit since it is merely a revaluation and no profit has yet been realized.

▲ **REVALUING ASSETS**
Sometimes an organization chooses to show an asset, such as a building, at a higher current value rather than at its original cost, and the difference is shown in a revaluation reserve. This informs the reader of accounts that the profit exists but cannot be distributed because it is, as yet, unrealized.

LOOKING AT LINKING STATEMENTS

Although the principle is that the retained profit must equal the increase in the balance sheet, often there is so much information that a linking statement is needed to clarify the situation. This statement sets out recognized gains and losses, and movement in shareholders' funds, and it reconciles the profit and loss account to the balance sheet. In addition to listing the retained profit for the year, this statement may detail gains and losses in currency fluctuations on foreign assets, issuance of additional share capital, and other technical items. In essence, shareholders' funds show how much money shareholders have chosen to leave behind in the business, which is all at risk should the business fail.

CHECKING FOR CLARITY ▶
Ask an accountant to guide you through a linking statement, showing why shareholders' funds have increased in the year.

USING CASH FLOW STATEMENTS

The cash flow statement is key to understanding how well cash, which is the lifeblood of a business, is being managed. Give this statement the attention it deserves, since the profit and loss account and balance sheet can provide only a part of the picture.

49 Remember the adage that profits are vanity and cash is sanity.

50 Bear in mind that profits do not repay loans – only cash can do that.

FOCUSING ON CASH

The third of the key financial statements, the cash flow statement, is practically the most important yet is often underused. When cash stops circulating, a business will die. The profit and loss account shows the profits made in the accounting period, but profits are not cash – and it is crucial to know how much actual cash has been received or paid out. The balance sheet shows the often large flows of investing activities, such as the purchase of fixed assets or the acquisition of a business, but it does not reveal whether the business has an excess (or lack of) cash. The cash flow statement links the other two key statements using cash as an objective, no-nonsense measure that is verifiable against the bank balance.

CASH FLOW STATEMENT

Operating profit		63
Depreciation		45
Increase in stocks		– 23
Increase in debtors		– 85
Increase in creditors		– 27
OPERATING CASH FLOW		– 27
Interest paid		– 20
Dividends paid		– 10
Exceptional costs		– 10
Taxation		– 16
Capital expenditure		– 85
CASH FLOW BEFORE FINANCING		– 148
FINANCING		
Increase in overdraft	60	
Decrease in bank loan	– 15	
Decrease in mortgage	– 5	
Issue of share capital	100	140
MOVEMENT IN CASH		– 8

◀ **REVIEWING A CASH FLOW STATEMENT**

Starting with operating profit, the statement shows how cash has been generated or consumed. It reveals aspects of a business that are difficult to gauge from the profit and loss account alone.

UNDERSTANDING THE PRINCIPLES

Cash flow statements generally follow a standard format and, while variations on the theme exist, similar principles are used worldwide in order to make the statement more useful and easily understood. The document is sectioned into meaningful blocks and subtotals, providing clear information on the cash movements within an organization's key activities. These include normal trading activities, interest and dividends, tax, investing activities, and financing. To understand the statement, you must know what is counted as cash. The generally accepted definition is that cash items are those to which an organization has immediate or one-day access, which means actual cash, bank accounts, and short-term deposits.

CULTURAL DIFFERENCES

Two attempts have been made by different countries to quantify just what a statement based on the flows of cash should contain. The first is the Source and Application of Funds Statement, but this was unclear about what was a flow of cash was, and has generally fallen out of favour. The second is a Cash Flow Statement, which more closely defines cash and produces an overall more meaningful document.

51 Manage your own working capital and control your cash aggressively.

52 Think of working capital as a sponge: it absorbs cash if left alone and releases it if squeezed.

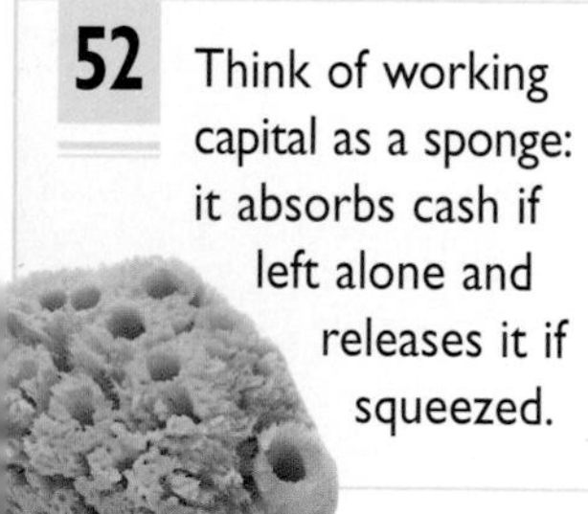

CALCULATING OPERATING CASH FLOW

The first and most important subtotal on the cash flow statement is operating cash flow, which shows how much is generated from simply trading. To calculate this, the operating profit (from the profit and loss account) must be adjusted. First, non-cash items, such as depreciation, which had already been deducted on the profit and loss, must be added back in. (Remember that depreciation is not – and never will be – a pile of cash.) Next, the working capital, or net current assets, from this and last year's balance sheet are adjusted, with the increase in stocks, debtors, and creditors being the difference between the two. If there is more stock now than a year ago, then cash must have been paid out. If debtors owe more, then they temporarily hold cash, so there is less in the business. If suppliers are owed more (because they haven't been paid), then the business temporarily has more cash.

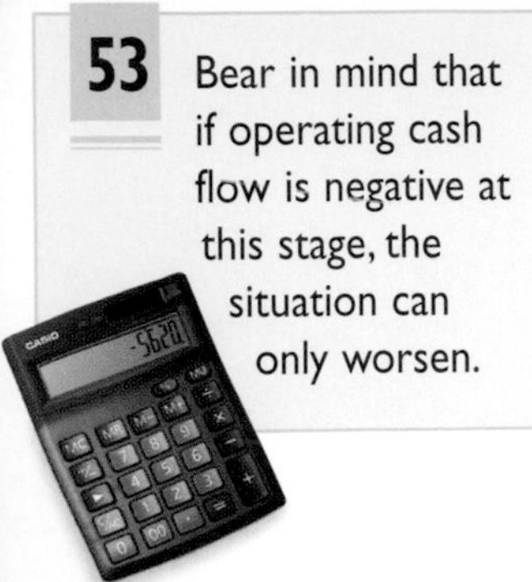

53 Bear in mind that if operating cash flow is negative at this stage, the situation can only worsen.

DETERMINING CASH FLOW BEFORE FINANCING

The subtotal of cash flow before financing shows how much the organization has either generated or will need to find to stay afloat. To calculate this, non-trading items such as interest, dividends, and tax must first be deducted or credited. Any interest paid or received in the year is shown, as are any dividends paid or received. The point is to reflect how much the organization is paying out simply to "service" its debt and share capital. Finally, taxation on business profits is deducted.

DETAILING CASH FOR CAPITAL EXPENDITURE

Once interest, dividends, and tax have been accounted for, then capital expenditure comes into the equation. Cash spent on purchasing, or received from the sale of, normal fixed assets is detailed here. If fixed assets are bought on hire purchase or leasing, then only the cash paid is shown. One-off items such as the purchase of a business are also shown. If an item is large compared to normal year-on-year cash flow and requires significant financing effort, this part of the statement reveals whether that item can be afforded or not.

54 Note that spending on fixed assets will often exceed profit.

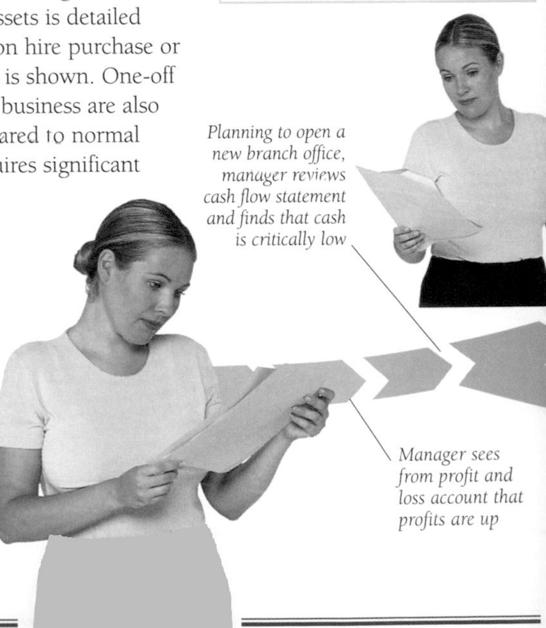

Planning to open a new branch office, manager reviews cash flow statement and finds that cash is critically low

Manager sees from profit and loss account that profits are up

KEEPING UP WITH CASH FLOW ▶

This illustration shows two possible outcomes to managing cash flow. A manager who looks only at profits may not even realize that there is virtually no cash in the business. A successful manager reviews the cash flow statement thoroughly before making any commitments and is able to prevent financial disaster.

MANAGING CASH FLOW

Controlling cash flow is management's prime financial task. It is critical that managers understand where cash flow comes from and how it is spent by an organization, since this can make the difference between financial success and disaster. When operating cash flow is negative, there are four levers that can be pulled to improve it: make more profit, decrease stock, decrease debtors, and increase creditors. These may not help, however, if an organization is expanding because growth inevitably means increasing sales, which results in larger debtors and stock, hence worse cash flow. This may be inescapable but must be recognized and planned for. Another key consideration is whether the annual dividend and interest bill is affordable. If not, does the funding of the organization need overhauling? Finally, buying certain assets may be entirely discretionary and should be carefully thought through before making commitments. Remember, cash is critical.

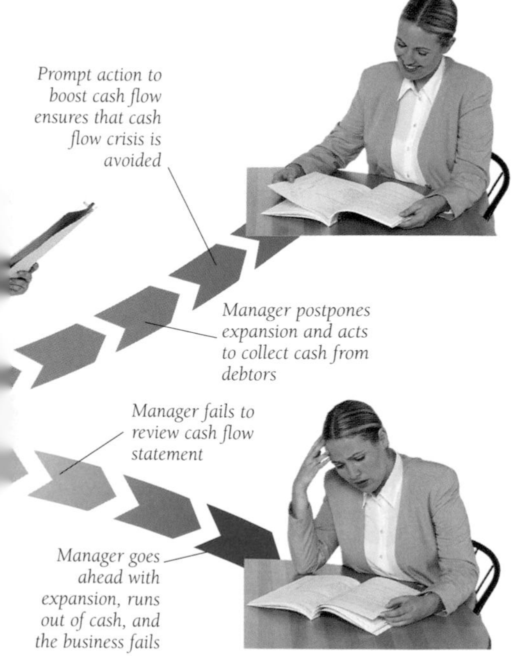

Prompt action to boost cash flow ensures that cash flow crisis is avoided

Manager postpones expansion and acts to collect cash from debtors

Manager fails to review cash flow statement

Manager goes ahead with expansion, runs out of cash, and the business fails

CALCULATING MOVEMENT

Two main sources of financing are debt (loans) and equity (share capital). Loans taken out or share capital issued are sources of cash; loans repaid or share capital repurchased are uses of cash. The difference between cash flow before financing and the sub-total of financing indicates the overall movement in cash for the year, which must agree with the difference between this and last year's cash in the balance sheet.

55 See that movement in cash and the bank account tally.

PRODUCING CASH FLOW FORECASTS

The forward-looking cash flow forecast is often forgotten because it is not required by law or regulations, yet it is an invaluable document. Use the forecast to help you predict cash flow in the future and keep an informed eye on your business.

56 Be aware that cash flow usually turns out to be worse than you plan for.

57 Remember to control capital spending properly.

58 Note that revenue and capital spending are often related.

ANTICIPATING PROBLEMS

Cash flow forecasting differs from cash flow statements in the perspective it adopts – it is forward rather than backward looking. Its purpose is to predict at what point the demands on an organization's cash resources become so great that cash is exhausted – whether from normal business demands or planned growth.

▼ **PRODUCING FORECASTS**

Involve colleagues regularly in forecasting cash flow. By planning in advance you can ensure you have the cash available for future commitments and solve problems before they arise.

Colleagues check timings of receipts are realistic, especially for new initiatives

Accountant ensures consistent assumptions about cash flow timings

Manager asks whether forecast capital spending plans are definite

USING A CASH FLOW FORECAST

Prepare a cash flow forecast from the profit and loss account and balance sheet. Working monthly, combine the anticipated amounts with cash flow timing predictions for each item of revenue and expenditure, remembering to include any likely one-off items. Then calculate the closing balance sheet, representing what is owed or owing from what you have not paid or received.

DO'S AND DON'TS

- ✔ Do be sensible about the timings of cash flows; they are often made more difficult by optimistic budgets.
- ✔ Do ask plenty of "What if?" questions about cash flows, should timings of significant amounts change.
- ✗ Don't assume that cash flow will not be a problem for you just because it has not been in the past.
- ✗ Don't presume that everyone will always keep to their terms about payments into or out of the organization.

▼ CREATING A CASH FLOW FORECAST

Extend the profit and loss account items and estimate the likely timings for each item. Add the predicted cash flow timings for each month to indicate cash surpluses or funding requirements.

Profit and loss account figures are divided into annual and monthly amounts

Timing of cash flow is estimated for the individual profit and loss account items

Actual cash receipts and payments are recorded for each month

PROFIT AND LOSS ACCOUNT			PREDICTION	CASH FLOW					
Item	Annual	Month	Payment	Jan	Feb	Mar	Apr	May	Jun
Sales	2,400	200	One month credit	0	200	200	200	200	200
Cost of Goods Sold	-1,800	-150	One month credit	0	-150	-150	-150	-150	-150
Office Supplies	-48	-4	One month credit	0	-4	-4	-4	-4	-4
Rent	-24	-2	One month advance	-4	-2	-2	-2	-2	-2
Salaries and Wages	-264	-22	Immediate	-22	-22	-22	-22	-22	-22
Selling and Marketing	-36	-3	One month credit	0	-3	-3	-3	-3	-3
Delivery	-24	-2	One month credit	0	-2	-2	-2	-2	-2
Heat, Light and Power	-12	-1	One month credit	0	-1	-1	-1	-1	-1
Interest Payable	-24	-2	Immediate	-2	-2	-2	-2	-2	-2
			Monthly cash flow	-28	14	14	14	14	14
Profit	168	14	**Cumulative cash flow**	-28	-14	0	14	28	42

Annual profit is calculated by deducting expenditure from revenue

Monthly total for cash receipts and payments is calculated

Cumulative cash flow is calculated, showing actual money in the bank

MEASURING PERFORMANCE

Ratios are essential tools for interpreting the messages behind lines of figures. Learn how to use ratios and how to translate supplementary reports for a clear view of business performance.

UNDERSTANDING RATIOS

A ratio is calculated by dividing one figure by another. Used logically and consistently, performance ratios can provide important indicators and highlight trends. Understand where ratios are useful and what they can reveal about performance.

59 Analyze profitability first, closely followed by asset efficiency.

60 Always look at performance ratios in the context of the business as a whole.

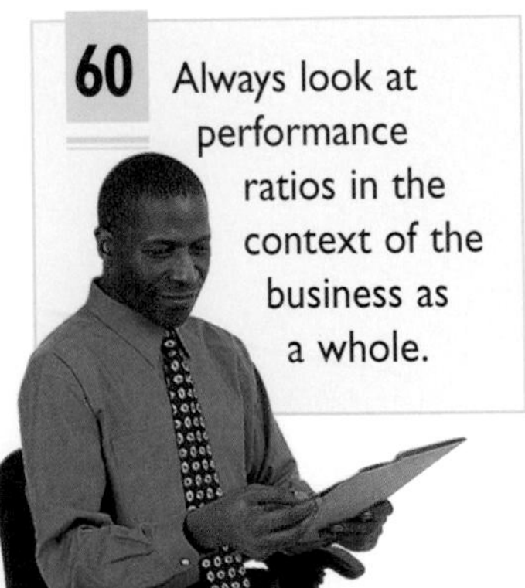

USING RATIOS

Ratios are most useful when produced and analyzed regularly to help identify important trends in areas such as cash and profit management. They can also be used to help make comparisons year-on-year and between organizations. However, since no two businesses are alike, this is fraught with practical difficulties. There are many ways of calculating ratios and there is no one correct method. Avoid relying on ratios alone to provide a full answer as to why one organization is performing better than another – you must examine the business as a whole.

61 Obtain sets of comparative ratios for your business.

62 Show ratio results graphically to help you spot trends.

ANALYZING EFFECTIVELY

When interpreting accounts, most people are interested in four key areas: profitability, efficiency, financing, and liquidity. Profitability measures how much income is made from sales, and is assessed by analyzing the profit and loss account; efficiency measures the use to which assets are put; financing shows the degree and affordability of funding; and liquidity measures whether there is sufficient cash to continue operating. Efficiency, financing, and liquidity can be evaluated by analyzing the balance sheet.

MEASURING ROCE

The most important overall ratio for measuring performance is called Return on Capital Employed (ROCE). This reveals how much profit is being made on the money invested in the business and is a key measure of how well management is doing its job. ROCE is calculated by dividing the operating profit by the capital employed (shareholders' funds plus long-term liabilities on the balance sheet). The rate of return should be higher than a shareholder could make by depositing their funds elsewhere, such as in a bank or building society. The ROCE also needs to be higher than the cost of borrowings, or a business will be paying more in interest than it makes on the money borrowed.

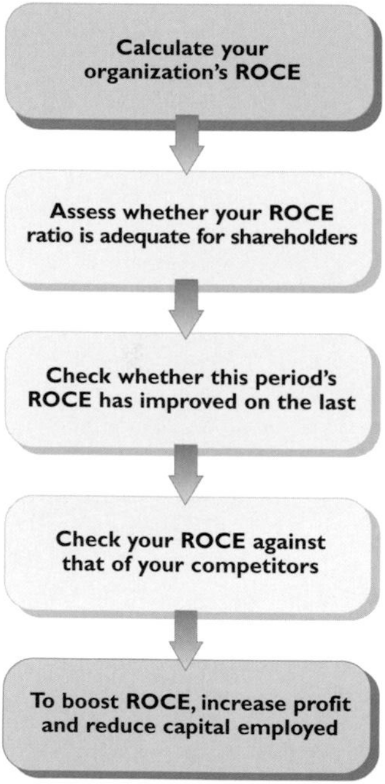

DO'S AND DON'TS

- ✓ Do use ratios that are appropriate to the nature, type, and size of the organization under scrutiny.
- ✓ Do take a balanced and holistic view of ratio analysis.
- ✗ Don't be hidebound and inflexible in your choice of ratios for assessing performance.
- ✗ Don't be too accurate about the results you calculate from accounting figures.

USING ROCE TO ASSESS YOUR PERFORMANCE

Calculate your organization's ROCE

↓

Assess whether your ROCE ratio is adequate for shareholders

↓

Check whether this period's ROCE has improved on the last

↓

Check your ROCE against that of your competitors

↓

To boost ROCE, increase profit and reduce capital employed

ANALYZING A PROFIT AND LOSS ACCOUNT

Line-by-line analysis of the profit and loss account provides a valuable insight into business performance. Find out what the figures really mean using a series of measures that show how profits are being utilized and determine whether they can be improved.

63 Always perform a quick top to bottom line review of profits.

64 Assess revenues and expenditures as a percentage of sales.

EXAMINING KEY LINES

Start by taking an overview. First, look at the top line of sales: are figures up or down on last year, and is any increase or decrease reflected in the retained profit on the bottom line? If not, examine the statement to ascertain where the profits have gone to. Use commonsense, look for obvious trends, and watch for factors that may affect your analysis; has the accounting period been a long one, for example? Then, to make year-on-year or industry comparisons easier, calculate each of the key lines as a percentage of sales. Known as common sizing, this strips out the effects of both volume and size.

USING COMMON SIZING ▼

Express each line of the proft and loss account as a percentage of the top line – sales. Do this particularly for gross profit, total operating expenses, operating profit, and retained profit.

PROFIT AND LOSS ACCOUNT
(INCLUDING RATIOS)

	CURRENT PERIOD	%	PREVIOUS PERIOD	%
Sales	2,200	100.0	2,050	100.0
Cost of sales	1,700	77.3	1,600	78.0
GROSS PROFIT	500	22.7	450	22.0
OPERATING EXPENSES	46	2.1	42	2.0
Office supplies	24	1.1	20	1.0
Bad debt charges	15	0.7	14	0.7
Rent	245	11.1	194	9.5
Salaries and wages	30	1.4	22	1.1
Selling and marketing	20	0.9	18	0.9

Salaries and wages as a percentage of sales has increased; find out why and take corrective action

65 Concentrate on operating profit, but also note what follows.

ANALYZING FIGURES ▼

Calculate ratios for interest payable, taxation, and dividends. Compare the current accounting period figures with the previous period to ascertain whether a business's health has improved or deteriorated, and pinpoint reasons why.

ASSESSING AFFORDABILITY

Interest payable, taxation, and dividends are not directly related to trading performance, but how easily an organization can afford to pay them is a key measure of its health. Assess the affordability of these items using specific ratios. First, divide operating profit by interest payable to work out how many times an organization could afford to pay that amount of interest (interest cover). Use the same method (PAT divided by dividends) to assess the affordability of dividends. Finally, divide taxation by profit before tax to give the apparent tax charge as a percentage, which should approximate to the official tax rate on business profits. Investigate any glaring discrepancies.

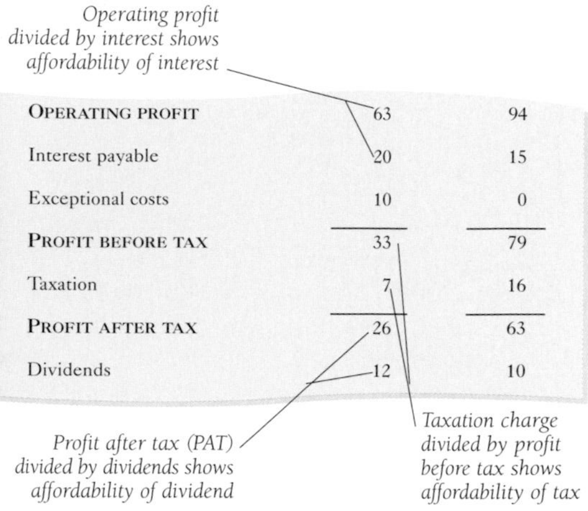

OPERATING PROFIT	63	94
Interest payable	20	15
Exceptional costs	10	0
PROFIT BEFORE TAX	33	79
Taxation	7	16
PROFIT AFTER TAX	26	63
Dividends	12	10

Operating profit divided by interest shows affordability of interest
Profit after tax (PAT) divided by dividends shows affordability of dividend
Taxation charge divided by profit before tax shows affordability of tax

EVALUATING PROFIT IMPROVEMENT METHODS

To boost profits, a well-run organization may use a profit improvement checklist. This is an accepted list of things to do in order of preference. Look at the following areas of the profit and loss account to gauge whether an organization has been putting this checklist into practice:

- Has it increased the selling price of products or services? (This could mean stopping any discounts, which would have the same effect.)
- Has it reduced the cost of sales (COS)? (This could involve either buying in more effectively or introducing more efficient business processes.)
- Has gross profit improved? (This would be the effect of taking both steps above.)
- Has volume increased? (An efficient organization would take this step only after assessing the profitability of its products and services to decide which items make a real profit.)
- Have selling, general, and administration (SG&A) costs been reduced?

READING A BALANCE SHEET

Another way of improving business performance is to reduce the amount of capital tied up in the balance sheet and increase the uses to which it is being put. Examine the balance sheet thoroughly to gain some clear measures of efficiency.

66 Note that figures in a balance sheet may be seasonal or unrepresentative.

67 Look at the notes to accounts to find the right figures to use.

GAUGING EFFICIENCY

Assess the overall efficiency of a business by measuring the number of times its assets (you can use fixed, current, or total assets) divide into the top line of sales. This is called asset turn and it shows whether more sales are being made with the same number of assets. On its own the ratio is meaningless but, when compared to the asset turn of previous years, it can indicate whether a business is becoming more, or less, efficient.

EVALUATING CASH MANAGEMENT

The amount of time that stock is held before being sold (stock days), how long customers take to pay (debtor days), and how long a business takes to pay its suppliers (creditor days) are classic efficiency measures. Using the stock, debtor, and creditor figures for the end of the current accounting period, calculate the number of working capital days. Then look for period-on-period trends and examine how the figures compare against the industry average. Too many working capital days can cause a cash crisis; too few mean that a business cannot operate properly.

▼CALCULATING WORKING CAPITAL RATIOS

To calculate working capital days, use the balance sheet figures and the two lines of sales and cost of sales on the profit and loss

Stock divided by COS x 365 gives stock days

Debtors divided by sales x 365 gives debtor days

Creditors divided by COS x 365 gives creditor days

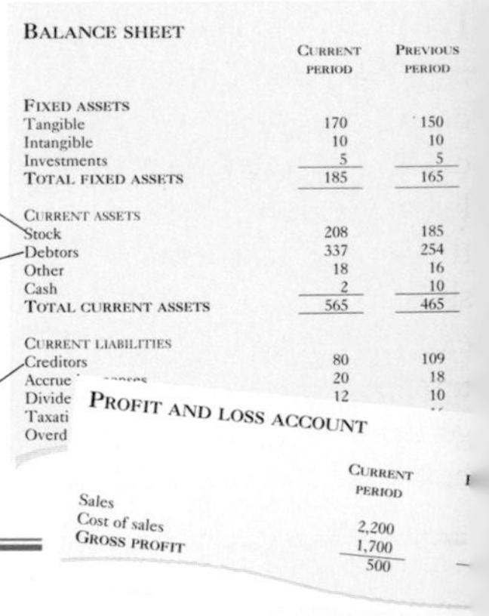

BALANCE SHEET

	CURRENT PERIOD	PREVIOUS PERIOD
FIXED ASSETS		
Tangible	170	150
Intangible	10	10
Investments	5	5
TOTAL FIXED ASSETS	185	165
CURRENT ASSETS		
Stock	208	185
Debtors	337	254
Other	18	16
Cash	2	10
TOTAL CURRENT ASSETS	565	465
CURRENT LIABILITIES		
Creditors	80	109
Accrue	20	18
Divide	12	10
Taxati		
Overd		

PROFIT AND LOSS ACCOUNT

	CURRENT PERIOD
Sales	2,200
Cost of sales	1,700
GROSS PROFIT	500

68 Calculate the cost effect of one extra day of debtors.

EXAMINING SOLVENCY

To assess whether an organization has enough money to cover its debts, or is liquid, there are two commonly used measures: the current ratio and the quick ratio (or acid test). To calculate the current ratio, divide current assets by current liabilities. Most textbooks suggest that the target for this ratio should be at least 1 or, in other words, that current assets should be greater than current liabilities. To calculate the acid text, divide current assets less stock by current liabilities, on the grounds that stock will not convert to cash quickly. When using these ratios, remember that businesses showing a ratio of less than 1 are not always a cause for concern. For a cash retailer, for example, nil debtors, low stock, and high creditors equal efficiency, not inefficiency, as such ratios might suggest.

▼ USING BALANCE SHEET RATIOS

The key balance sheet ratios of fixed asset turn, working capital days (stock, debtors, and creditors), and current and quick ratios are calculated to measure efficiency.

BALANCE SHEET RATIOS

	CURRENT PERIOD	PREVIOUS PERIOD
FIXED ASSET TURN	11.9	12.4
Stock days	44.7	42.2
Debtor days	55.9	45.2
Creditor days	(17.2)	(24.9)
TOTAL	83.4	62.5
CURRENT RATIO	3.16	3.04
QUICK RATIO	2.00	1.83

Deleting stock from current assets in the numerator will reduce the ratio, but it will still be comfortably more than 1

Dividing current assets by current liabilities gives a ratio comfortably more than the target of 1

69 Remember that the popular current ratio has its limitations.

ASSESSING FINANCING

Lenders and investors in particular like to assess how long-term financing is structured, since an organization that borrows heavily is riskier than one that has borrowed little. The key ratio used is known as debt to equity, or gearing. To calculate this, divide long-term liabilities by total shareholders' funds plus long-term liabilities, expressed as a percentage. For example, if long-term debt is £70 and shareholders' funds £30, gearing is 70 per cent. There is no target figure here; instead closely monitor trends.

70 Assess whether a business is properly financed and structured.

UNDERSTANDING INVESTORS' RATIOS

The world of the stock exchange and external investors uses its own ratios to determine the viability of a business. These hard-nosed measures can be very revealing, so learn how to assess accounts from an outsider's point of view.

71 Note that investors focus on performance within industry sectors.

72 As with all financial analysis, always look at more than one ratio or measure.

DETERMINING WORTH

A stock exchange index is a list of the largest quoted companies on the stock market as measured by their overall worth, or market capitalization. Whether you work for a quoted company or want to know how competitors, customers, or suppliers are performing, market capitalization gives a crude estimate of a company's worth in the marketplace.

CALCULATING MARKET CAPITALIZATION

Market capitalization is calculated by multiplying the number of shares that the company has issued (a finite, known figure) by the share price (a fluctuating figure). Share prices are irrelevant on one level because the price at which they are traded will not affect a firm's daily production or selling routines. However, the market's perceived worth of a company may well affect its ability to borrow or raise more funds from the investment community.

◀ **LEADING THE MARKET**
Companies in stock markets are ranked according to their total worth, with the highest valued businesses forming that country's stock market index (such as the Dow, FTSE, DAX, and CAC).

LOOKING AT PROSPECTS

The price earnings (PE) ratio provides a good indication as to how the market views a business's prospects. To arrive at this ratio, first calculate earnings per share (the profit that each share has generated) by dividing profit after tax (from the profit and loss account) by the number of shares that have been issued. Then divide the market price per share by earnings per share to give the PE ratio, which reveals how a share is currently valued compared to the profits that it made last year. A high PE ratio is a sign of confidence in a company; a low PE ratio indicates the reverse.

Pay particular attention to what the price earnings ratio tells you.

▼ **WATCHING THE FIGURES**

Investors and interested parties use the financial press's figures of corporate performance to see how key organizations are performing and to make comparisons between similar business types.

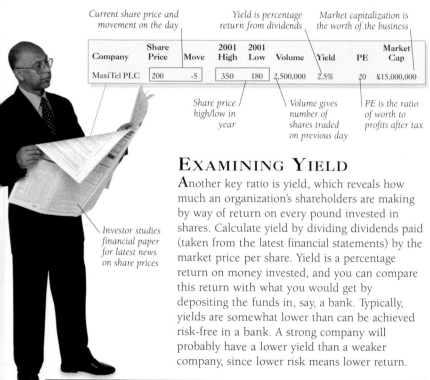

Current share price and movement on the day

Yield is percentage return from dividends

Market capitalization is the worth of the business

Company	Share Price	Move	2001 High	2001 Low	Volume	Yield	PE	Market Cap
MaxiTel PLC	200	-5	350	180	2,500,000	2.5%	20	£15,000,000

Share price high/low in year

Volume gives number of shares traded on previous day

PE is the ratio of worth to profits after tax

Investor studies financial paper for latest news on share prices

EXAMINING YIELD

Another key ratio is yield, which reveals how much an organization's shareholders are making by way of return on every pound invested in shares. Calculate yield by dividing dividends paid (taken from the latest financial statements) by the market price per share. Yield is a percentage return on money invested, and you can compare this return with what you would get by depositing the funds in, say, a bank. Typically, yields are somewhat lower than can be achieved risk-free in a bank. A strong company will probably have a lower yield than a weaker company, since lower risk means lower return.

GATHERING MORE INFORMATION

In addition to the key statements, large organizations disclose a wealth of extra information, either voluntarily or because they are legally obliged to do so. Know where to look for these details and what you can glean from them.

74 Get to know what is contained in a published report and accounts.

75 Examine reports and notes carefully; you may uncover some very important details.

INTERPRETING AUDITORS' CODE

The role of auditors is to report on whether financial statements have been properly prepared in accordance with company law and GAAP. Rather than stating that accounts are correct, however, they choose such phrases as "give a true and fair view" or "fairly represent", which mean that these accounts are said to be "unqualified", or clean. Watch out for "qualified" opinions, as these point to areas where there is either uncertainty or, more worryingly, disagreement.

UNDERSTANDING QUALIFIED PHRASES

PHRASE	EXAMPLE	MEANING
"SUBJECT TO"	"Subject to continuing support from its bankers..."	Without the bank's support, the business will fail.
"EXCEPT FOR"	"Except for the valuation of certain stock items..."	There has been a fundamental disagreement between the auditor and management about a matter.
"DO NOT"	"The accounts do not..."	The accounts have not been properly prepared.

READING THE DIRECTORS' REPORT

When annual accounts are published, a company's directors often comment on the results. Since there are strict laws on disclosure, whatever is said must be objective rather than propaganda-led. Pay attention to the section on salaries (companies today are sensitive about what they pay their directors, since salaries must be seen to be commensurate with overall corporate performance) and look at details on share options. Both sections provide clues as to how well the directors think that they and the company have done in the year.

76 The larger the organization, the greater the scope for information.

COMPARING REPORTS ▶

In their report, directors generally outline how they expect the organization to perform in the coming year. Most will be optimistic to reassure shareholders, but watch for cautious qualifications or predictions of a "tough year ahead".

77 Read the reviews by key directors for optimism about prospects.

78 Dig into the notes for interesting further details and information.

FOCUSING ON NOTES TO ACCOUNTS

Copious notes are attached to the main financial statements of balance sheet, profit and loss account, cash flow, recognized gains and losses, and movement in shareholders' funds. It is important to read these in conjunction with the actual statements. While the notes to accounts may appear daunting at first, persevere with them because they are an integral part of the message and must be understood. Domestic and housekeeping items, such as important dates for the diary and a timetable of the annual general meeting and immediate future events, are also to be found in the notes.

Broadening Your Knowledge

The complexity of accounting means that "grey" areas abound. Learn where anomalies arise, how accountants deal with them, and how to improve the quality of your own internal accounts.

Exploring International Issues

Many organizations today operate on an international level, yet, despite increasing globalization, accounting practices and formats still differ significantly around the world. Understand the differences to help you pinpoint where problems can arise.

79 Always be clear about on which rules the accounts are based.

80 Accept that profits and assets can vary significantly between countries.

Highlighting Problems

Accounting measurements are dependent on the rules of individual countries, and this is often a hindrance to international business transactions. Investors must negotiate cross-border obstacles, multinationals face differences in profits concepts and taxation, and governments creating trading blocks face unequal opportunities and economic distortions. As a result, efforts are being made to reduce differences through harmonization.

DEFINING DIFFERENCES

Because countries have different legal systems, taxation regimes, historical influences, and business practices, their accounting systems are also different. Continental Europe's strong legal framework of accounting plans and commercial codes contrasts with the UK and US combination of legal principles and a separate set of accounting rules. Some countries require the figures in financial accounts to be the same as for tax purposes, while in other countries no connection is needed. Political and historical factors also play their part, with much of the world influenced by the UK system. The need for open information for shareholders has ensured that appropriate financial statements have evolved.

81 Get to know the key international differences that affect you.

▼ EVALUATING SYSTEMS

Countries influenced by the UK and the US tend to have a more pragmatic approach to accounting, the onus being to inform shareholders. In other parts of Europe and in Japan, strict taxation and legislation rule out any subjectivity or deviation, so that accounts are less useful and informative to interested outsiders.

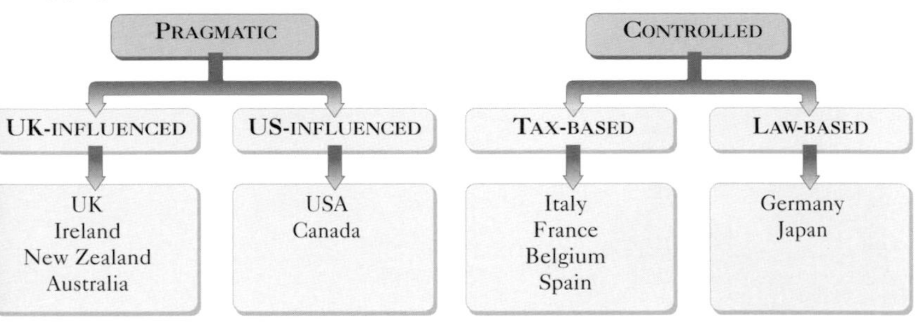

HARMONIZING ACCOUNTS

Since accounting systems around the world measure items such as assets and profits differently, international comparison and analysis are difficult. As a result, there has been mounting pressure to harmonize accounting. For ten years, an international accounting body has been working to produce International Accounting Standards (IAS). These now provide the benchmark worldwide and are used by many multinationals, some of which even prepare two versions of accounts. One version will comply with General Accepted Accounting Principles of the country in which the organization is based, and another will be in accordance with IAS. The EU is a useful example where law-based harmonization has taken place but no GAAP convergence has occurred.

LOOKING AT COMMON PROBLEMS

Accounting is technical by nature and there are many complex issues facing accountants. As a manager, there is little to gain from poring over technical details, but it is useful to know where problems can occur and how they can be dealt with.

82 Grasp the essentials, not the details, of technical accounting.

83 When dealing with unfamiliar technical issues, seek advice from an expert.

LISTING LEASED ASSETS

One type of fixed asset that causes controversy is a leased asset. This is an asset that a business uses for three years or more but that it does not legally own (unlike all other fixed assets). At some point in the future, annual lease costs may be substantial, but organizations prefer to omit this liability from their accounts to avoid giving the impression that they are borrowing more now. Accountants prefer to treat a leased asset as if it were owned in order to give a fairer picture. The debt can then be shown on the balance sheet for all to see.

CONTROVERSIAL INTANGIBLE ASSETS

Goodwill and brands can cause controversy (see pp.26–27), and other intangibles can do the same:

- Patent (an object or process patented by someone else and bought by a company). The amount paid for the patent is written off over the period of time for which it has been acquired.
- Know how (similar to a patent but the object or process purchased may not have been formally registered).
- Copyright and intellectual property, typically on music and books.
- Research and development. Costs are taken out of the profit and loss account and shown as an asset in the balance sheet. If this is the case, current profits and assets may be overstated.

MAKING PROVISIONS

When the cost of a future event, such as a reorganization, will seriously hit profits, an appropriate figure must be deducted from the current year's profits. This is known as making a provision and is a way of alerting users of accounts to what lies ahead for the organization. If an impending event may potentially hit profits (perhaps there is a threat of legal action, for example), it is often not included on the financial statements but should be noted in the accounts as a contingent liability. Finally, if an event with significant financial impact should occur between the balance sheet date and the date of signing off accounts, this must also be noted.

POINTS TO REMEMBER

- You should try to form an opinion on the financial health of an organization.
- Provisions have traditionally been devices for "smoothing out" the fluctuations in profits.
- It helps to appreciate the principal accounting logic behind each technical treatment.

ACCOUNTING FOR GROUPS

Gleaning useful information from the accounts of a group of companies, where some businesses are controlled by others, can be a difficult exercise. Accounts should give a picture of the whole business entity, but that picture may be blurred if, for example, the holding company has been juggling with the figures of one of its subsidiaries. As a manager, you will probably be interested in the performance of other companies in your group, as well as in the group's performance as a whole. Accounts of groups of companies are sometimes called "consolidated" accounts.

▼ UNDERSTANDING GROUP ACCOUNTS

Subsidiary companies produce their own accounts, which are incorporated into those of the parent company to give more meaningful results for the group as a whole.

Parent company prepares the accounts for the entire group

GROUP HEAD OFFICE

Company directors pass individual sets of accounts to the parent company

Individual company prepares its own accounts separately

COMPANY A | COMPANY B | COMPANY C

RECOGNIZING CREATIVE ACCOUNTING

An accountant is expected to present a company's figures in the best possible light, while being accurate and truthful at all times. Learn to recognize when the figures are being manipulated, since this is a sure sign of creative accounting at work.

84 Recognize that one person's smoothing is another's creative accounting.

85 Check if creative accounting is increasing or suppressing profits.

WHY HIDE THE TRUTH?

Every organization has its own agenda for creative accounting: the larger company wants to report bigger profits, the smaller to pay less tax. Being creative need not involve adjusting figures: merely choosing an accounting date to paint a rosy picture, extending an accounting period to bolster profits or confuse the picture, or failing to file accounts at all are popular ways of hiding the truth.

REVIEWING PROFITS

On the profit and loss account, watch for a high number of invoices at the year end, which is a method of boosting profits. Similarly, postponing invoicing until the start of the new accounting period ensures that tax is payable later. Depending upon whether a business has had a good or bad year, it may lower income by recognizing too many costs, or raise it by not recognizing enough. To determine disproportionate activity, look at the first month of the next accounting period: discrepancies will usually be compensated for here.

▼ **SMOOTHING THE RIDE**
Making profits is unlikely to be a smooth process, so a creative accountant will smooth out peaks and troughs to show a steady, well-managed line of profitability.

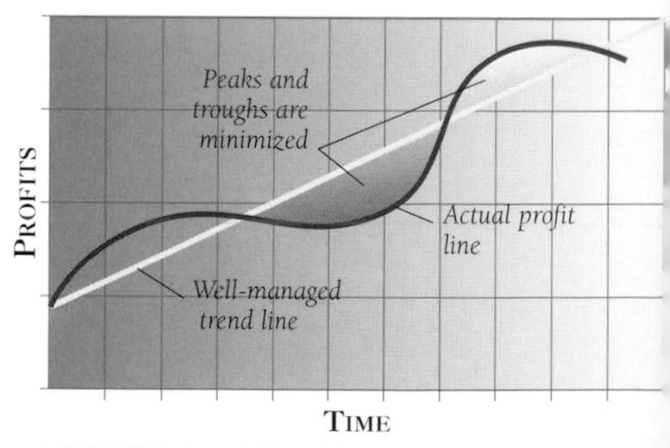

COOKING BOOKS ▶

Accounts can be based on books and records that might range from being lightly cooked to completely burned. But the task of the reader to distinguish between what is acceptable and what is simply going a little too far will always be difficult, since creatively produced accounts will always look normal on the surface to the untrained eye. Always seek technical advice if you suspect that anything is not right with the figures.

CASE STUDY

Happy Nappies wanted to increase its profits, and decided to use some typical creative accounting techniques. First, it recognized revenue on sales earlier: on confirmation of order rather than on delivery of goods, thereby increasing sales revenue. Second, it reduced costs by taking out of the profit and loss account expenses relating to a new factory and adding them to the factory's costs – again increasing profits and the balance sheet. Third, it extended the depreciation lives on certain high-value assets, again increasing profits and the balance sheet. Finally, it changed the method for translating the value of foreign-located assets into domestic currency, again manipulating the value of its balance sheet. Not all of these treatments are within the spirit of accounting law and practice, but they are commonplace nevertheless.

TAKING STOCK

On the balance sheet, the first item to watch is stock. If its value is too high, stock on the balance sheet (and profits) will be too high. Look at creditors as well: managing working capital efficiently involves stretching creditors (suppliers), but within reason. Payment of bills may be postponed before the year-end, increasing creditors and giving an impression of a good relationship with suppliers who are willing to extend credit. Check the first day of the next accounting period to see whether large cheques are subsequently despatched to suppliers.

86 Remember that the balance sheet and profit and loss move together.

▼ CHECKING THE BALANCE

Remember the principle that when profits increase, so does the balance sheet. Think of two ends of a dumbbell moving in tandem, so that what affects one statement will also affect the other.

Undervaluing closing stock results in higher cost of sales and lower profits

Undervaluing closing stock gives a lower balance sheet stock amount

BENEFITING FROM MANAGEMENT ACCOUNTS

The fact that management accounts need not follow any rules makes them usefully flexible but more open to error. Recognize the uses and drawbacks of internal accounts and how you, as a manager, can improve the information they contain.

87 Remember that management accounts lack standardized rules.

88 Understand the purpose and use of management accounts.

UNDERSTANDING MANAGEMENT ACCOUNTS

Prepared and distributed internally within an organization, management accounts are governed by the needs of managers. They are used to help keep control of, and make decisions regarding, the everyday running of a business. As a result, they often contain more than mere financial information. They generally focus on four main areas: past scorekeeping, present problem-solving, present controlling, and future planning.

COMPARING EXTERNAL AND INTERNAL ACCOUNTS

EXTERNAL ACCOUNTS	INTERNAL ACCOUNTS
Are published externally and available for the public.	Are distributed internally within an organization and kept confidential.
Must conform to legal requirements and GAAP principles.	Are not bound by any rules or regulations, and may follow any format.
Are generally published once or twice a year and look backwards at the past year's results.	Are produced on a regular basis and focus both on previous and future periods' results.
Reflect the financial reality of what has happened in an organization.	Provide a means of controlling the financial side of an organization now and into the future.

DRAWING CONCLUSIONS

A striking feature of management accounting is that, having been liberated from the usual accounting format straitjacket, endless different layouts and formats can be used. Unfortunately, because there is no one correct way of producing these accounts, there is considerable room for error. But how can you gauge the accuracy of your management accounts? A useful exercise is to attempt to reconcile the internal figures to the external financial statements, since the external ones will be inevitably be more accurate. If internal accounts differ seriously from the external statements, there is cause for concern.

89 Try to reconcile internal to external accounts.

90 Examine your company's internal accounts package.

▼ **INFORMING MANAGERS**

The content of management accounts should reflect what managers want them to show, namely how well the business has performed according to plan, and what corrective action, if any, should be taken.

The current month's actual figures are compared to the budget

The year to date is perhaps a better indicator of long-term trends

MANAGEMENT ACCOUNTS FOR AUGUST

ITEM	MONTH				YEAR TO DATE				FULL YEAR
	ACTUAL £	BUDGET £	VARIANCE £	%	ACTUAL £	BUDGET £	VARIANCE £	%	FORECAST
Sales	195	200	-5	-3	1,520	1,600	-80	-5	2,300
Cost of sales	-150	-150	0	0	-1,190	-1,200	10	1	-1,770
Office supplies	-5	-4	-1	-15	-35	-32	-3	-9	-53
Rent	-2	-2	0	0	-16	-16	0	0	-24
Salaries and wages	-21	-22	1	5	-166	-176	10	6	-250
Selling and marketing	-4	-3	-1	-33	-30	-24	-6	-25	-40
Delivery	-2	-2	0	0	-18	-16	-2	-13	-27
Heat, light, and power	-1	-1	0	0	-8	-8	0	0	-12
Interest payable	-2	-2	0	0	-16	-16	0	0	-24
PROFIT	8	14	-6	-43	41	112	-71	-63	100

Actual results are compared to budget and expressed as a variance

Variance is also expressed as a percentage

A forecast is made for the full year's results

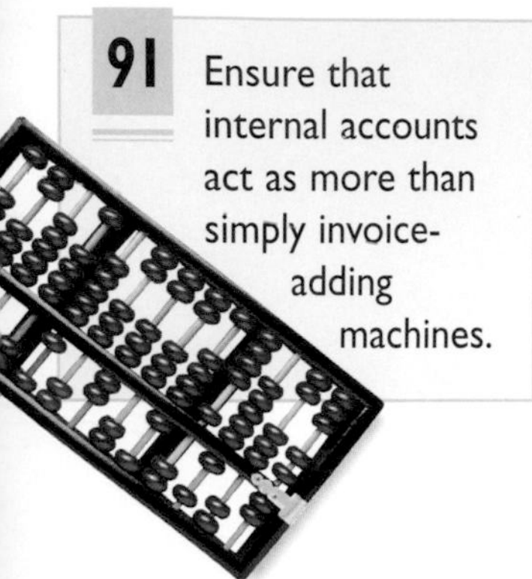

91 Ensure that internal accounts act as more than simply invoice-adding machines.

ASSESSING QUALITY

The quality of management accounting varies considerably. Even large, successful organizations can produce poor management accounts. Yet it is vital for managers to have financial documents in excellent user-friendly shape. Your accountant is bound to feel happier giving you a traditional profit and loss account – it is, after all, what he is used to. But this will not always contain the information you need to help you to manage your business into the future. If your management accounts are sub-standard, take steps to improve them.

IMPROVING EFFECTIVENESS

As a manager, it is important to take a more enlightened view as to how well your company is performing. This involves moving away from accountant-dominated management accounts toward those that are tailored specifically for you. Think of the quality of management accounts as a spectrum. At one end of the spectrum are traditional accounting statements, midway along are accounts containing targeted management information, and at the opposite end are manager-led accounts containing indicators tailored specifically to your particular needs. Make sure that your organization is evolving in the right direction.

92 Take responsibility to improve management information.

Manager looks for practical measures that will help him in the future

Accountant suggests showing information graphically for greater clarity

ASKING FOR INFORMATION
Ask your accountant what information is available internally that will help you in your role as manager, and discuss ways of presenting that information to make it easy for you to use.

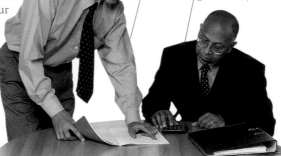

USING PERFORMANCE INDICATORS

To ensure that the information you receive from accountants is valuable, consider using a set of measures known as key performance indicators (KPIs). These can be whatever you want them to be, provided that they are important to you and your organization. Generally, KPIs will include a financial component in their calculation, but this may not always be the case. Typical KPIs could be made up of the following: sales per employee, cost of sales per customer, marketing costs per new customer, labour cost per pound of sales revenue, and percentage of leads converted into sales. Often KPIs can lead on to league tables of performance internally.

▼ BRAINSTORMING MEASURES

Sit down with your fellow managers and decide which indicators would be most valuable in helping you to monitor and improve your performance.

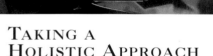

Manager invites group to make suggestions for appropriate performance indicators

POINTS TO REMEMBER

- Your traditional financial accounting information should be up to date and bullet-proof.
- The measures you take should be meaningful to you in your role.
- Developing a package of easy-to-obtain management information with your accountant will help you manage your department.

93 Consider using scorecard-type performance measures.

TAKING A HOLISTIC APPROACH

Just as some say that a business should be measured on more than its financial results, it is also necessary to use more than one performance indicator. A popular management information tool, the balanced business scorecard sets out the following four cornerstones for measuring performance holistically:

- Customers: Are we pleasing them? Are they coming back? What is our market share?
- Internal business processes: How can we improve processes to serve customers better?
- Learning and growth: Are we equipped to deal with customer and business process demands?
- Financials: How is the organization faring financially? The scorecard suggests that if the first three aspects are right, this will be, too.

MAKING FUTURE FINANCIAL DECISIONS

For a business to succeed, it must focus on using accounting concepts and techniques that look to the future. Set an example by basing your calculations on the right costs and using simple but effective tools for sound financial decision-making.

94 Remember that future-looking decisions require new financial skills.

ADOPTING A NEW MINDSET

To make the right accounting decisions for the future, you need to rethink the way that you look at figures. Rather than rely on the backward-looking perspective of the past, accountants, organizations, and managers must learn to adopt a new, forward-looking mindset. Traditional accounting uses historic costs and bases all analysis on those figures. However, when looking at decisions into the future, simply adding up the figures will not give the right answer.

95 Accept that future-looking decisions of most companies are flawed.

COMPARING PAST AND FUTURE ACCOUNTING NEEDS

PAST	FUTURE
Traditional accounting uses historic costs and what has happened in the past.	Future decisions ignore sunk costs and what has already happened.
Traditional decision making uses the concepts of profit and return on assets.	Future decisions use the concepts of incremental cost and opportunity cost.
Traditional measurement treats all money as being of the same value – whenever it arises.	Future decision-making looks at discounted cash flows rather than simple profits.
Historic accounting arrives at a simple result of pounds profit.	Future-looking decision-making compares projects and the option of doing nothing.

IGNORING SUNK COSTS

Getting the costs right is paramount to correct decision-making. A golden rule is to always ignore "sunk" costs, or those that have already been paid and cannot be recovered – hence sunk. Although someone will try to allocate blame for what has been spent, you should reject it as a cost when assessing whether to go ahead with spending in future. How often do you hear, "We have to go ahead because of all the money spent so far"? This is a common yet potentially calamitous approach.

96 Compare the cost of doing a project with the cost of doing nothing.

FOCUSING ON INCREMENTAL COSTS

Costs that are incremental are those that increase or decrease – the point is that they do in fact change – as a direct result of something taking place, hence the term incremental. If a project uses two people for a month and there are none available internally, then you will have to buy in people from outside; this is a true incremental cost. If, however, people are available internally and you use them, there is no incremental cost to the business as a whole, so these are not relevant costs. The rule is to ignore irrelevant costs and count only incremental costs.

97 Only costs that are incremental to a company as a whole are relevant.

▼ COUNTING COSTS

There are three golden rules to follow when considering which costs should be taken into account to help you make a decision on future spending: ignore sunk costs, disregard irrelevant costs, and count only incremental costs.

Money spent on hiring Tom to conduct market research could not be recovered
Alice was asked to take over the project as well as continue with her own projects
Peter was recruited from outside the organization to finish the project
PROJECT
SUNK COST
IRRELEVANT COST
INCREMENTAL COST

98 Ask your accountant what the cost of money is to your company.

99 Be aware that future cash flow predictions need not be accurate.

USING SIMPLE MEASURES

Once the costs are right, consider whether the outlay will be worthwhile using measures known as accounting rate of return and the payback period. To calculate the rate of return, simply add up all the figures and express them as a percentage. For example, an outlay of £1,000 with returns of £400 for the next three years gives a profit of £200, or a return of 20 per cent (about 6 per cent per annum) on the initial investment. Then assess the amount of time taken to recover the initial outlay – the payback period – which in this case is two-and-a-half years. Acceptable payback periods vary from six months to several years, depending on your organization and its view of the future.

APPLYING DISCOUNTING

When making decisions about the future, it is essential to recognize the time value of money. The example of a £1,000 outlay providing returns of £400 per year over the next three years is misleading, since the £400 will be worth a different amount in the first, second, and third year. To add together future sums of money fairly, you must first discount a future sum back to its value today, or "present value". Assuming a 10 per cent interest rate, £1 in one year's time is worth only 91p today (91p plus 10 per cent equals £1). The value today of 91p in one year's time is about 83p. Multiplying cash flow by the discount factor gives the discounted cash flow, or DCF, and the sum of them is called the net present value, or NPV.

▼ CALCULATING DISCOUNTED CASH FLOW

Multiply the amount of the cash flow by the discount factor to give discounted cash flow. Add down to give the sum of all the discounted cash flows, or net present value (NPV). Normally, a project will be undertaken if its NPV is positive.

Cash outflows typically happen at time 0; inflows occur annually thereafter

Total anticipated future cash flows are estimated

Discount factor will typically be around 10%

TIME	CASH FLOW	9% DISCOUNT FACTOR	DISCOUNTED CASH FLOW
0	£–1,000	1.00	£–1,000
1	400	0.92	368
2	400	0.84	336
3	400	0.77	308
TOTAL	£200		£12

Sum of all the discounted cash flows gives the NPV

AVOIDING PITFALLS

There are some drawbacks to be aware of when using discounted cash flow:

- Timescale: for how many years should a project run? (The longer it runs, the better it will look.)
- Accuracy: predicting future events will always be difficult and subjective, especially when projected several years.
- Significant figures: keep it simple and do not try to get too much unrealistic accuracy into predictions.
- Cost of money: use actual cost, average cost to the organization, or even a "hurdle" rate in order to sleep at night.

USING A HIGHER FACTOR

Applying a higher discount factor will make future cash flows more attractive and a project appear more viable. There will be a point (or discount factor) for a project where the NPV is £0. The discount factor that gives a NPV of £0 is called the "internal rate of return", or IRR, and is approximately the project's inherent profitability. NPV and IRR both point to the same conclusion, but many people prefer the easily compared IRR because it is expresssed as a percentage.

100 Use spreadsheets to check your calculations when discounting.

101 Remember your decision is only as good as your estimated figures.

▼ USING INTERNAL RATE OF RETURN

A 9% discount factor gives an overall project NPV that is just positive. A higher discount factor will give lesser weighting to future cash flows, so the figures are reworked using a discount factor of 9.7%. This factor gives a NPV of £0, which is the IRR of the project, or its inherent profitability.

Timescale same as for previous example

Individual undiscounted cash flow amounts are unchanged

Since the NPV was positive at 9%, a higher factor is used

TIME	CASH FLOW	9.7% DISCOUNT FACTOR	DISCOUNTED CASH FLOW
0	£–1,000	1.00	£–1,000
1	400	0.91	364
2	400	0.83	332
3	400	0.76	304
TOTAL	£200		£0

Revised NPV is 0%, so 9.7% is the project's IRR

ASSESSING YOUR ACCOUNTING SKILLS

A knowledge of accounting practices and the three key financial statements will ensure that you can interpret and use the information supplied in any set of accounts. Use this questionnaire to test your understanding. Answer the questions as honestly as you can. If your answer is "never", mark Option 1, and so on. Add your scores together, and refer to the Analysis at the end of the questionnaire.

OPTIONS

1 Never
2 Occasionally
3 Frequently
4 Always

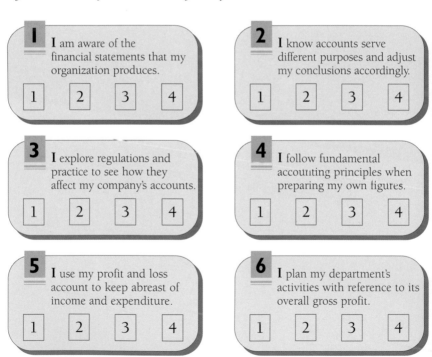

1 I am aware of the financial statements that my organization produces.

1 2 3 4

2 I know accounts serve different purposes and adjust my conclusions accordingly.

1 2 3 4

3 I explore regulations and practice to see how they affect my company's accounts.

1 2 3 4

4 I follow fundamental accounting principles when preparing my own figures.

1 2 3 4

5 I use my profit and loss account to keep abreast of income and expenditure.

1 2 3 4

6 I plan my department's activities with reference to its overall gross profit.

1 2 3 4

7 I understand what operating profit contains and how to interpret it.

1 2 3 4

8 I refer to retained profits as the key measure of growth potential for a business.

1 2 3 4

9 I explore my balance sheet to investigate how to become more efficient.

1 2 3 4

10 I closely assess my capital expenditure amounts by analyzing fixed assets.

1 2 3 4

11 I am aware of the meaning and impact of intangible assets.

1 2 3 4

12 I refer to the type and amount of current assets to manage working capital.

1 2 3 4

13 I pay attention to whether stock and debtors are long-standing.

1 2 3 4

14 I consider the impact of the amount of debt and its repayment date.

1 2 3 4

15 I examine shareholders' funds to see how a business has grown.

1 2 3 4

16 I understand the difference between profits and cash.

1 2 3 4

17 I analyze the cash flows that my organization generates.

1 2 3 4

18 I plan my department's future with reference to a cash flow forecast.

1 2 3 4

19 I use only accounting ratios that are specific to what I want to understand.

1 2 3 4

20 I express all lines in a profit and loss account as a percentage of sales.

1 2 3 4

21 I have certain preferred balance sheet ratios that I use and fully understand.

1 2 3 4

22 I understand the external investor ratios commonly used in stock exchanges.

1 2 3 4

23 I read the supplementary disclosure statements in my company's annual accounts.

1 2 3 4

24 I am aware of how key international differences in accounting affect me.

1 2 3 4

25 I accept that I will need to seek help with some technical accounting issues.

1 2 3 4

26 I consider how creative accounting may have influenced the figures.

1 2 3 4

27 I refer to management accounts to help me control my department's finances.

1 2 3 4

28 I seek to improve the content and quality of internal financial information.

1 2 3 4

29 I realize that I must use different financial criteria in making future decisions.

1 2 3 4

30 I use discounted cash flow to appraise the financial viability of a project.

1 2 3 4

31 I recognize that accounts contain certain subjective and flexible elements.

1 2 3 4

32 I learn from and continually improve upon my accounting analyses.

1 2 3 4

ANALYSIS

Now that you have completed the self-assessment, add up your total score and check your performance. Whatever level of success you have achieved, there is always room for improvement. Identify your weakest areas, then refer to the relevant sections of this book, where you will find practical advice and tips to help you establish and hone your accounting skills.

32–64: Your understanding is not as thorough as it should be at manager level.

65–95: You are reasonably proficient in your understanding of accounting. Make renewed efforts to improve areas of weakness to ensure better results from your accounting skills.

96–128: You are a highly competent user of accounts. However, do not become complacent: keep using your accounting skills by practising them regularly.

INDEX

ACKNOWLEDGMENTS

Dorling Kindersley would like to thank the following for their help and participation in producing this book:

Photographer Matthew Ward.
Photographic assistance Silvia Bucher.

Models Tracey Allanson, Phil Argent, Jeanie Fraser, Mark Fraser, Aziz Khan, Kaz Takabatake, Dominica Warburton.

Make-up Evelynne.

Picture research Anna Grapes, Andrea Stadler.
Picture library assistance Melanie Simmonds.

Indexer Hilary Bird.

PICTURE CREDITS

Key: *a* above, *b* bottom, *c* centre, *l* left, *r* right, *t* top
The Stock Market Philip Wallick 25; **Superstock Ltd** 35*t*, 48;
Telegraph Colour Library 4–5.

AUTHOR'S BIOGRAPHY

Stephen Brookson qualified as a chartered accountant with KPMG and went on to work for Ernst & Young before setting up his own management and training consultancy. He has presented seminars and training events in many countries, and he is the author of *Mastering Financial Management* and *Managing Budgets*.